Spearpoint

Spearpoint

"TEACHER" IN AMERICA

Sylvia Ashton-Warner

 VINTAGE BOOKS

A Division of Random House, New York

VINTAGE BOOKS EDITION, MARCH 1974

Library of Congress Cataloging in Publication Data

Ashton-Warner, Sylvia.
  Spearpoint; "teacher" in America.

  Autobiographical.
  1. Ashton-Warner, Sylvia. I. Title.
[LA2317.A8A3 1974]   371.1'00973 [B]   73–14780

ISBN 0–394–71997–2

To American Teachers

I shall not be out there among the stars.

—JULES LAFORGUE

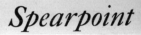
Spearpoint

The futuristic peaks below and now more desert below the space song of the plane . . . a monopolizing monotone. As voices are with no lilt in them when feeling is deceased: no cadences of emotion. As words are with no flash from them when temperament is quenched: no inspiration of imagery. Colorless, bloodless, polysyllabic abstractions spoken for the sake of speaking. Thoughts which make me wonder why I've come so far on a matter of education.

Mountains, canyons and again more desert, until there ahead erupts a city as from the earth itself: angularly concreted and pale in the sun like cities in Mediterranean latitudes long since lost, their day of affluence over. It must be time to come down to land now, but as the plane whirs lower I'm reluctant to forsake the imagery in mind of yesterday's cities, of space-people and of eartheners . . . the long-legged beauty of the spaceners, the hairy simplicity of the eartheners . . . for it's always hard to descend. As hard as it is to see why these asked for me.

The down-to-earth metal fact of a car as people come to meet me, the rock reality of the terrain as I'm driven up into the mountains, the piercing peaks of the heights as we climb in altitude, the tender gold of the autumn aspens and the great yellow house where I'm to live alone . . . continue to make me wonder why they sent for me, for a person like me, to lead their education. Why not choose a North American pedestrian, with degrees from here to there lashing behind, who, weighted down with the lead of multisyllabled platitudes, could be counted on not to lift from the ground for any reason at all, least of all on the wings of imagery, but to follow faithfully and determinedly the preorganized paths of premeditated perpetuations? Why call on me . . . a child?

One day in the autumn, I go straight from the plane into a foreign school of a culture I thought I knew. I'm agog with confidence in my own work, knowing it like ABC, but not knowing that I, from the tail end of civilization, have descended upon the spearpoint. True I have lived in other countries at varying stages of civilization, so that I know what civilization is and what a stage of civilization is, but here, in no time, the days are a matter of survival and my work is XYZ. There's no time space or mind space to remember romantic conceptions of life about being a wandering exile or to dream about the stars. My comfortable principle of life . . . "Ask of no man but give to all" . . . fails in the face of survival. My new watchword, clumsily assembled, becomes . . . "Adapt and survive."

A parent drives me round to see the school, which turns out to be the physics building belonging to the Humanities Institute, something you could be excused for mistaking for a spaceship by the outside look of it: a sort of long, narrow, rocket-looking shape landed temporarily on the plain, about to disappear any minute on its way somewhere into the immensity of the galaxy.

Carrying in mind a picture of a former infant room in which the organic work first arose . . . a picture of a room, wide, tall, and wall-less, I enter the front hatch to find inside a long, low-ceilinged double row of cabins . . . well, rooms if you must . . . divided by a tunnel corridor, with one cabin for the cockpit and another at the stern. Beneath the crowding voices of children I hear the muted boom of the furnaces like the engines warming up.

I stay awhile to get the hang of it all, but the air in the ship, if you can call it air . . . overaltituded, light on oxygen . . . the dreamlike unreality and the intoxication makes me think of outside. Where are the windows and doors? Yes, there are windows closely shut, and the front door through which we came in, but the cabins have been designed for quiet physicists testing theory against theory, not thinking about how to get outside as I do or as the children may be.

But how beautiful the children are! Long-legged, slender-torsoed, and with faces straight from the ads. "Hullo, little one," I say.

"I'm not little."

"Oh? How old are you?"

"Four."

Less than an hour is more than enough. Outside on the plain between the mountains, I think, Adapt and survive. As for the dream I had, it's gone.

The school has been born but one week only, and is making grunts like primitive man. Teachers have barely arrived and don't know the children, children themselves are newcomers and don't know the teachers, and teachers don't know each other, like a crew hired the night before. Nor is there known any common philosophy, none of us having had time to talk, other than the idea of an open school. I myself could have done with a year's preparation, but Fate doesn't like preparation and looks round for a crisis like this and for me when he finds himself bored.

There is no headmaster, director or commander of the spaceship, since all are equal . . . this much of a philosophy is established early . . . and parents take turns for the day in the office, which to me, prepared or not, appears successful. They're competent, kind, purposeful people who'll do anything for you. Very early in the chaos, I learn to like this and turn to them for everything except teaching techniques. For teaching techniques we'll turn to each other, the staff being a composite headmaster. In theory excellent, but in practice there's no time. Too many problems crowd by the hour like fragments of shattered glass in a lunar module damaging pressure suits . . . with no Mission Control to solve it.

My part is to implant a new kind of learning in this new kind of school, the organic style in the infant room. Except that no one has told me so. "Why don't you give us a lead?" asks Carl.

"Who, me? Why me? Aren't we all equal?"

"You're the director of this end."

"Me? Am I?"

"Yes, you. We're all hanging round waiting for you to give us a lead."

"Interesting. I didn't know."

So I'm the director of the infant room but must not direct, as all are equal. Irrespective of how much one has learnt and thought, how long one has lived, how much experience one has clocked up, I'm told that no teacher likes any other teacher to be above him and no child likes any teacher to be above him, from which I read that equality means that none can be above the least and laziest. Authority turns out to be a very dirty multi-letter word indeed, though all very sweetly implied in the kindliest and sincerest voices and which I learn at once. Direct, please, but don't direct. "What about picking up your blocks, Henry?"

"I dowanna."

"You used them. Come on. I'll help you." Kneel and start.

"I said I dowanna and I don have to."

Where do you go from here? "Well, who else is to pick them up?"

Long legs planted firmly apart, he looks me contemptuously in the eye: "Not me, you dum-dum!" and sticks out his tongue for emphasis. So he wins, for we are equal. Equality on board appears to mean inverted authority. There's authority here but not from me.

Instead of easing into the school happily and confidently as I'd expected, I find myself engaged on all fronts, alarmed: exploring a new culture with no compass, colonizing new lands of thought and action without equipment, climbing new mountains of education without ropes and pickaxes, warily rounding new heights; my only nutriment the charm of the teachers and parents, my only fuel an alien's survival. How do you direct yet not direct? Even the words "coax," "advise," or "suggest" are *persona non grata* in the vocabulary of the spaceship; even the word "request." To a young volunteer teacher, "Would you please bring in the children?"

She clicks her heels to attention and salutes.

I go and call the children myself. The only acknowledged difference between me, teachers and children is that I have the misfortune to be older, having committed carelessly the indefensible offense of aging. Generation gap is all over the place, yet not, as the young suppose, between the youth of the holy present and the old of the unholy past but, which they don't know, between the youth of the present and the future, for I am the future in disguise. This generation gap is not a matter of a few decades between the Now and the Then but a matter of several hundred years between the Now and an era hence. For this is where the thoughts of a young French poet of the nineteenth century and of mine abide . . . in the palpitating silences of clusters of stars interweaving their rounds. Not grounded in the hackneyed present.

The only way I see to direct and yet not direct is to teach by example and hope for the best, so that I return to the daily round I'd completed thirty years ago when I was young, when I was strong, intent and lured by a dream. Down I get on the floor with the children, from half past eight till three. Not that I mind being on the floor with our children; I'd rather be there for the present and forever, for you don't get bored among children, never knowing what they're going to say or do; and besides this is my level anyway, being a child myself, though professionally I'm surprised at the sudden demotion.

The stars, it is certain, will one day meet.

—JULES LAFORGUE

I weave among the aspens with a borrowed walking stick and between the cradling mountains, staring aloft at unknown birds and down on the unknown flora. Out on the plain between the heights, I breathe in air and dimension. Horizons tall glance down on me, but not with contempt, which is a big distinction between man and nature and makes you like nature. The purple up there and the golden aspens beam indulgently, sharing their color with the meadow plain blooming around my feet. Firs in the distance, spruce and pine and trees they say are cottonwood, the whole impartiality of nature, her classlessness, calming as I return to the big yellow house and softening the ways of Fate.

Yet I'm not thinking of Fate or mountains, birds or flora, or about the firs and spruce, but about my subject: the mind of our child. About the organic work I've come here to do.

Organic work is not new but as old as man, as old as that first animal-man who stood erect from apehood. His grunts were not for nothing, they meant some want or fear: guttural utterances which were the captions to the pictures in his hairy mind, symbols of the images of what he needed for self-preservation and for racial preservation.

Survival imagery first . . . water and food; imagery of what he feared . . . enemy, thunder, famine. Then racial imagery . . . woman, children. The urgency of his feeling about these needs forced the pictures from his mind into his throat and out upon his tongue to communicate them to another.

The pictures in his mind are part of his mind as an organ is part of his body, as indispensable to the life of his mind as the heart to the body, as the kidneys, stomach and lungs. His feeling, combusting in imagery, is a functioning organ, which is the reason I call it organic. You hear me talk of organic writing or the organic shape of a morning, and since it is from his feeling that his imagery arises, is born, I call it native imagery. When working with fermenting ideas, like yeast, you've got to create new terminology as you go along. His native imagery is what blows up from his instinctive feeling; his sentiment, hates and fears, from his passionate desires. There's no telling what you find in the undermind if you allow it to live.

The presence in his mind of this living imagery I call the third dimension of his personality . . . for my own convenience really, so that I can see it. You have the length and breadth, the surface area; then you get the depth, the deep places of the undermind. Simple to see. It is claimed that I am too simple in the way I see a thing, but then so are children. Children and I are no good at abstractions, but like to see a thing, and as it happened I never grew up myself. I did have a period of supposed adulthood, but that adulthood is now bracketed in dream and I am a child again, so how can I see or say the abstract? Which is what I like about the company of children, not knowing what they're going to say, what *we* are going to say, and when we do say it we understand each other. Spare us the pages of impenetrable terminology from universities in textbooks and graduates, long words with many syllables yet carrying no picture; and from the textbook psychology of the young. Handy slogans on older people they learnt on page 97 without themselves having lived that far. To return to my point of departure: I call the life of the imagery the third dimension.

Our feeling is the force which compels us to think, to talk and try to do things, like the fuel which propels a car. Without this third, we are two-dimensional, flat, without contour; we're like a car without any gasoline left on the side of the road; we can't *go*. Like a desert with no well of water; we can't *grow*. Without feeling, we can't think and do things. We believe we can think and do, we actually think and do, but we are only a copy of others and God knows there are enough copies around. Our thought and action are not our own, not organic.

We are born with feeling. Like the grunts of primitive man, our utterances are revealing. Organic education is concerned with these . . . the captions of our feeling.

.   .   .

I don't know why I've said, "The stars, it is certain, will one day meet," nor am I sure what he meant, but what we do have in common is that we both write in exile and both are possessed with the future. Strange having to reach back to the nineteenth century to find youth possessed with the future . . . why not here and now? Not just the immediate future either of hundreds of years only, but the future of man in the cosmos on one of our many habitable planets in the millions of solar systems in our galaxy. Living over a hundred years later in the age of science and technology, one has access to facts not available then to Jules LaForgue, such as the amino acids found on some meteorites, but his vision could fly further into the great innocence of the eternal suns.

Nevertheless this image makes its way from the under-mind out into my hand that writes in its wantful way: a picture of man's destiny in the firmament. What kind of education will we need to qualify us for that, I wonder? The only style of education I know flexible and mobile enough to keep up with the swiftly evolving point of civilization, with the astonishing mutating of people, is the organic style; for whatever our children are, their working material comes from them, from the spearpoint of civilization, from the middle traditional body and from the tail end of civilization where the young are returning to nature. Why have we forgotten the first learning of the first man, ignored the organic nature of our imagery? Why do we murder it daily in schools? Don't we want to stay alive? Are we in such a frantic hurry to take off mutated from the Earth forever? Maybe we are. Maybe we wish to be exiles from the Earth.

"The stars, it is certain, will one day meet," whatever LaForgue meant by that. Whatever I mean by repeating it. But the imagery is not noted for discipline. All will be done without me, it is certain. I shall not be among the gentle stars.

The professional formula—"Release the native imagery of our child and use it for working material"—remains timeless, changeless and axiomatic, but the application of it needs constant variation. Here, in no time, I'm reminded that a formula which suits one country well does not necessarily suit another, not without certain tailoring. Children differ profoundly from country to country, and our children differ again, bafflingly so. Not only will the manner of working with the native imagery need to be fitted to them, inch by inch, pin by pin, but where is their native imagery anyway?

Nor is it wholly a matter of our children learning; as an alien and a child, I am learning myself. Not just relax and enjoy a new culture as I do in other societies, but get down to business and study it. At all costs, try to understand it. Why are our children so quarrelsome and fretfully discontented? Why don't they play outside? Why don't they ask questions, for crissake? Surely they have curiosity? Why do they not cooperate one with another, work in pairs and groups interested in each other? Why don't they rush to play with the water? Where is the love of song, the rhythm in their comely bodies; how can they sit motionless with the guitar beating, and with Carl singing?

Before teaching anyone else, I must teach myself, whereas teaching oneself takes time. As I round strange corners in the mountains on my walks, short of air in the altitude, greeted in a friendly way by dogs . . . humanly sympathetic dogs . . . I re-examine my time with differing children in other parts, other colors, other conditions of the world: from Montessori flourishing in a Buddhist temple school in the thick of India, through the vitality and imagination of children in Israel, to Dickens relived in Mauritius, to the shining crisp black children in the back streets of London, to mention but a few . . . sorting out the distinctions and the likenesses, if any, and I keep a mood-by-mood watch on this new panorama, intent on adapting myself. Intent on surviving, to be accurate. Hoping to see out my apprenticeship. "Their graves are scattered far and wide," my mother would quote wistfully, "by mount and stream and sea." I will not be among the stars. Where will my grave be?

Tonight I may die. Rain, wind, sun
Will scatter everywhere my heart, my nerves, my marrow,
All will be over for me. Neither asleep nor awakening.
I shall not have been out there among the stars.

—JULES LAFORGUE

I'm having trouble with the dream I brought of a former infant room; I cannot relate it at any point to what I find here. The tiny cabin rooms like ivory towers, and now there's a door in the room at the stern which I'm pleased to call my room, where I'm to be found anyway, which the others call the meeting room and which the older children, as well as our young ones, use freely as a highway outside. But I'm not concerned about all this, for already the dream I brought is changing form to adapt itself to these conditions. Who knows? These ivory towers may turn out to be an advantage.

The parents taking daily duty in the office at the bow of the ship turn out to be an advantage, too. "Anything you want, Mrs. H. Anything at all."

"We need a sand table, sand in it. And a water tank, not

too high. And we need a long easel to accommodate five children each side, this long. And everything needs to be on casters so we can wheel them around. I could do with some blackboards on the walls, this low for the children. Up the other end of the ship—I mean building—I noticed large sheets of very good blackboard, in the cloakroom. Could some of it be cut into little boards for the children? I need supplies of clay and containers for it. This high. And I need an endless supply of soft cardboard, soft enough to cut with a scissors for the Key Vocabulary. I'd rather have timber ends for building than blocks—and oh, yes, some chalk. A lot."

"Chalk? What for?"

"For the children on their blackboards."

"Chalk," writing down. "Chalk is not looked on with favor in this country. The dust. . . ."

"I've lived through it so far. And you don't get so much paper piling round. God, the paper!"

"One of our parents will be in this morning, if you tell him what you want and give him the measurements of everything. Is there anything else?"

"Did I say paint?"

"The paint is here."

"Brushes and all that?"

"Yes, and a roll of paper."

"I wonder if I could have a low chair, please."

"We'll see to that. Anything else, just let us know. Anything."

"Thanks so very much."

There's not only my dream on the go but the school's too. Dear me, the size of the collective dream: in the teeth of opposition a perfect open school, providing both learning and freedom. Of course I've seen the freedom part, if this is what

22

in called freedom and we should show that we'll be more serious

it can qualify its freedom a bit. I'll see some learning too.

My word, there is something I forgot to ask for: a place for teachers to go for a retreat from this freedom. A place where one can make the tea and sit a moment in peace; at least a place to make the tea, if not a place to sit. I'm impressed indeed by what they call freedom among the incoming children, but less impressed by the freedom for teachers. Impressed even less than that by the concern for teachers as people. Wait a minute . . . are we people? Do we have feet that tire, throats that dry or senses with a human limit? Perhaps we don't. Something else to learn. I'm already learning that children are the lords of creation whose desires and whims are law. Well . . . it's something to have some kind of law. Quite something to know where you are.

Oh, the size of the dream, the dimensions, the multiplying accumulating bulk of it! With the weight of twenty atmospheres.

"What we really need," I say to Carl, cross-legged on the carpet, "is a system of jobs for which each is responsible. One for the pencils, one for the papers, another for the chalk and so on." From the children all over him, Carl smiles up at me. His eyes behind the glasses smile, his beard smiles and his whole long folded body is a long folded smile, from spare ears to bare feet. "You can't do that, Mrs. H.," he says. "Each owns his things. Each looks after his own."

"I can't say I've noticed it, Carl."

"That's what we do."

"Owning is one thing, looking after it another. Who's to know which-pencil-is-which sort of thing?"

He should be able to answer, "They keep them in their

desks," but there are no desks. Not only because there is no room for tables but also because "desk" is a four-letter word from the public system.

"They're all exactly the same," I continued. "And who has used what. And these children are only five, mostly, and I don't see their servants with them. What about the things we all use: blocks, books, paints, and soon there'll be sand, water and clay and blackboards and . . . It goes like this: each one needs to be responsible for some one thing. Responsibility comes into this, to the equipment. We really need this list of jobs."

"They won't like it" is all he says.

"But these mine-yours sequences go on all day."

"That is capitalism."

"Oh? But the concern of possession oversteps the substance."

"Capitalism," gravely.

"Capitalism takes time."

"So do jobs."

"Good answer."

A little girl is wrapped round his neck like a scarf, possibly short of a father. "Well, leave me out of it, Mrs. H."

"Oh, I'll do it."

"But that will be to assume collective ownership."

"Does that hurt children?"

There's much more to say, but this is not the time. The time was before school started, for at least the length of the summer, but teachers met each other only on the day school started. Opened, I mean, not started. Only the engines have started, and the countdown. "Rocky, please pick up those pencils."

"They're not mine."

24

"Gelo, will you pick them up, then?"

"I didn't use them." Finish.

All the teachers are on the floor with the children, since there are no chairs and because it looks more equal, but I stand at the BB, having a job to do. "So," after explaining it to those who are listening, "who will be the pencil girl?"

Odile says, "Me," with a smile too. Her proportions are straight from Fairyland and all that's missing is wings.

"Pencils," I print on the BB and beside it "Odile." And look at it. Fancy someone agreeing to do something! "And you need to count them each day, Odile, to see if you've got them all. Who will be the book people? Two."

"Me," from Peter, dark eyes glowing. Very dark eyes and a dimple, and snuggling between the knees of an American teacher. Other children nestle up to the teachers on the floor, though there are better attitudes of attention. If I were other than a groping alien, I'd see to this attitude of attention. Rapport between teacher and children has priority in learning, but listening is not unknown. There's a time and place for snuggling and nestling and a time and place for listening, but I have much more to learn myself before making the distinction; all I have really learnt so far is that everyone is equal. Not the nature of equality itself, which is different in this country.

"Here's Peter, a book boy," I print on the BB. "But two are needed for the books." Watch out, Mrs. H. That might be an order.

"Me, too," from a face and legs. A smile on long legs like Carl, and what a face and what legs; the physical beauty of these children!

"What's your name?"

"Durla."

"Peter and Durla the book people," printing her name. Praise God for willing people disposed to give a hand, whatever the motive. I take a second look at these two who still have living imagery. I'll remember them and see how their work goes later. There should be a relation between this and that.

But from Jonathon wistfully, "Isn it snack time yet?" Man eternal.

"Now the chalk. Who?"

The young American teachers on the floor covered in children. Pleasant for the children but less for the jobs. "Who will be the chalk boy?"

No answer. They don't know chalk. America goes the paper way. Goodbye, forests. A somersault from Gelo, long-legged and fair. All these long legs could be a case of inbreeding . . . if you know what I mean. As he upends, he pulls another with him. "I wanna go outside."

"Can we have our snack?" from Jonathon. I note Jonathon on account of his name.

"Monty, you can be the chalk boy."

"I dowanna," from the King of the Wannadowannas, a leading lord of creation.

"Why not?"

"I don have to, that's all," with an authority I could do with myself, confirmed by a roll on the carpet.

"Why don't you have to?"

"Jus because I dowanna job." Wanna, wanna, wanna, dowanna; excellent words for a song.

"But you use the chalk."

"I didn this morning. I was playing with blocks."

Any five-year-old can floor me in debate. Brains and legs

is the whole story. "Well, what about being the blocks boy?"

Irritated authority, "I said I dowanna job. I said I don have to. I can do what I like."

"Really?"

"A-huh."

"Interesting. I suppose you've brought your servants with you."

No answer. A pause while he thinks. He's tall for five, Monty, and fair as most of them are. You often hear his voice above the others, yelling his way through, and he doesn't get on with all.

"Who do you think you are? Who's going to look after your things if you don't, Monty?"

I think this has not occurred to him.

"Who are Carl and I?" I ask.

He thinks, then he answers, "Teachers."

"As long as you don't mistake us for servants."

He examines this idea.

"Snack," moans Jonathon. "I hate meeting."

"I'll do the chalk," from Durla, which makes two jobs for her.

"All right. Two for Durla. Now the blocks. We need two."

No offers. As it happens, they build very little. The teachers look sad and bored except Carl, who finds amusement in it.

But I've had enough of this "Who will . . . ?" business. Without the audience of the American teachers, this would have been over long ago. "Jonathon, you often play with the timber. You can be one of the blocks boys."

"No, I wanna have my snack," which is the thing about

Jonathon. He's got a mind that no one can push off its rails. Think of this mind engaged on something like getting onto Mars; nothing would stand in his way. Stand in his way? Float in his way. Meteors would change direction.

"You can have your snack when you've helped with the blocks." Mind or no mind, on or off course to Mars, this wannadowanna is a law of man, not of life, and it's life that's ahead of him.

But he has the perfect answer. His mouth trembles and tears come, and a tender teacher embraces him. He wins also.

"What about you, Gelo; will you help Jonathon with the blocks?"

"No." Flat. "See-see, when it's time to do the blocks," he argues lucidly, "I'm often busy doing something else. An-and sometimes when I'm not doing something else, then I'm doing something else. An-and I usually don't play with the blocks. It's better if the ones who played with the blocks, if they put them away. I-I shouldn't put away something I didn't use if someone else used it. I like to put away my brush if I'm painting and put away my own clay. But today I don't use the blocks and see I don't like to put them away." Rolls on the floor to get over the idea of putting things away, his legs straight upward.

Suddenly I've got an ally. Not from the teachers but long-haired Angela, with a face from heaven, who is seven. "Yet someone else," she accuses, "puts away your pencil and books and stuff: Odile and Peter and Durla."

Gelo pulls Monty upon him, laughing. "No," conclusively, "I like to put my own things away."

Another ally. "But you didn't yesterday," from Durla.

"Well, choose a job, Gelo," I say

"See, I like to do the clay when it comes. I like to make things with clay."

"Gelo for the clay when it comes," printing. "We need two on the clay."

"Me, me!" from Candy. "I'll do the clay," wrapped round Carl's neck. "With Gelo," she adds. So that's it. At least sex survives.

"Candy and Gelo," printing. "And back to the blocks boys. I'll tell you who the blocks boys are; they're Monty and Jonathon, so think that over." By God, this is naked authority. Watch it. Americans can't stand it.

In time we get to the end of the jobs, mountain time. Not so different from Maori time, which means you do things how you wanna if you wanna when you do them at all. Charming, modern, way out and all that. "All right, little ones—sorry, big ones, now we'll get our jobs done, then go to snack."

"I wanna go now," from you-know-who.

"Those who don't work don't eat," and that's a law of life.

In no time, the jobs are done and not so badly either, leaving a simple alien to ponder on the point that remains lying round, not put away. Instinctively I move to the window, open it a slit for air and look out over the plain to the mountains. It's a point that has something to do with everything from capitalism to equality, from authority to freedom, and nothing about the substance: education. Even if there were silence in a cool thinking place, I could not work it out, but with the room a high freeway again through the doors . . . To some bigger boys from up-ship, "Do you have to use this way all the time to . . . Can't you use the foyer door?"

"We have *every right* to use this door."

I retreat to the storeroom nearby and stand among the trash cans, to the muted boom of the furnace and in the difficult air, under the illusion I'm alone for a minute. But no one is alone in the storeroom, where the best conversations take place, while another aspect of the point surfaces: do teachers not matter as people? I could do with a cup of tea and a chair and a moment of privacy to think . . . to see if I could find education itself.

I look at my watch and count the hours ahead before I can disembark.

I'm sitting in silence over a solo meal in the big yellow house: a castle with six bedrooms and three bathrooms and a reception room nearly as large as my own at home, housing a grand piano better than mine at home. All for just little me. Lent for me at no rent for a few months, all of which itself is a statement of some kind; what? An act of faith in a new kind of school by one under no obligation. There's no boom of a furnace, no trash cans, no crowds and no high frantic freeway through the room, and I find my own thoughts again. Fragmented thoughts, fragmented vision, but my own at least.

Why think, anyway? Why teach at all? Why try to preserve the third dimension of a young personality? Who will want a rounded and full personality out there among the stars; on some distant planet at some distant time, stabbed by the spearpoint of civilization? Because it protects a man's originality so that he stays as interesting as he was when he was born? Not wholly. Because it's natural for him to think

and my mind do what he wants to? Not necessarily. It's because . . . since feeling is alive . . . the pressure of it
makes him act. If its passage outward is blocked in some
way, his native desires denied too much, frustration could
breed hatred.

The love he is born with could change to hatred, the
pictures in his mind become images of hatred, his thoughts
words and actions become captions of it . . . could. The
imagery of love could be replaced by the imagery of hostility,
pressed into his throat and over his tongue to be communi-
cated to others. He would still have feeling to make him go,
but it might be the way of hatred, which does not build but
destroys.

Not that I find any hatred here in our new kind of
school, not a sign of it. I find quarrelsomeness, discontent,
unwillingness and rudeness to a degree I've never encoun-
tered before, but I do not sense hatred. I've known far more
naked hatred in small children in other parts of the world.
But I don't sense love here, either. What's happened to the
dynamo of feeling; where is the third dimension? Why don't
they think and do things, rather than loll on the floor between
the knees of teachers; why don't they *want* to do things, why
can't they grow, why don't they *go?*

It's time to get going on the Key Vocabulary to find out
things for myself, in the teeth of trash cans, freeways, indis-
ciplines, opposition and the reigning wannadowanna. Somehow I'll work my way through it . . . circumvent the ruling
ogres striding from one end of the ship to the other: Authority and Equality. Fancy wasting energy and thought on these
damned obsessions. Let's forget them, for crissake, and find
education.

,　　.　　.

About twenty of the five-year-olds—fives, I call them—in the reception class, none in the second, none in the third, and about nine in Grade 2. In the organic shape of the morning, children of about seven would be the fourth movement, but since these particular nine children have had no previous organic work, they are not a fourth movement; they remain Grade 2.

Which brings me to the use of the word "grade" on living children. We grade fruit, meat, wool and eggs in my country, inanimate products without a mind, without the capacity to change, whereas I don't see a group of small children as mindless and changeless, with no need for movement and unity. Neither do you. It is more in keeping with the nature of man to call their progressions movements, as in a symphony in which one movement is part of a whole, one movement leading organically into the next, the whole four together making a statement on the climate of the soul of man. Did I say soul? Forgive me. Soul belongs to the residue of eartheners who'll be left here in the future, in their caves, under trees and hunting their food, taking all day to make love to each other and physically killing one another. Soul is the owner of the house in which the mind lives, when it does live, peering out the windows of the eyes.

Where was I? The organic shape of the morning has four movements, the first the reception class, where our most skilled teacher receives the new ones. The head of the infant department—or director, if you like—I see as the conductor, unifying, leading, and inspiring.

About twenty of the fives in the reception class with our relaxed Carl, not unfamiliar with letters. Some can make and recognize a few, but they tend to use capital letters found be-

fore school, picked up from TV or from books in shops. Less
hindrance than inconvenience. In learning the letters used in
all printing, they have something to compete with, but it
doesn't matter. If there's anything more adaptable than an
unrepressed child, it could only be a mirror. But I do still
wonder why people teach young children in capital letters before they come to school. Do you think they can't see or something?

Twenty or more on the Key Vocabulary . . . the K.V.,
we call it. Captions of the action and pictures in the mind of
our child. As the pattern of any physical movement is from
the body outward, so is the flow of the K.V. from the mind
outward, from the inside out. The words start often with our
child's own name, but not necessarily, or Mommy and
Daddy, then his brothers and sisters, even if there are nine-
teen of them in the family, which you find in some pill-less
societies—and more than that too here and there—by which
time he moves to people outside the family, things outside,
animals, pets, his bike. Not all run true to this route, of
course . . . man is unique and variable . . . besides, big
emotional explosions can take place in the course of it, but it's
a natural guideline.

I like the picture of the mind of our child as a house owned by
his soul, inhabited by his instincts; his wants, fears, desires
and loves, his hates and happinesses. A merry, motley, moving company, some potential homicides, others pure saints,
rubbing shoulders and elbows with one another, all together
going for it, like a carnival of celebrants dancing madly. At
times, from the pressures within, they venture outside into
the street for a breath of fresh air, exercise themselves and

encounter others, bring back food and something new to talk about, returning somewhat civilised.

But now you see the unskilled teacher outside in the street come to the door, not knock and wait, but gate-crash with his own company of imagery, join battle with the defendants, rout them and take over occupancy, so that the native images flee and hide under beds, behind doors, beneath the staircase or in the toolshed at the back, where they die of wounds and deprivation. The house is now full of alien imagery belonging to the teacher. What's wrong with it . . . it's imagery, isn't it? But the thing is that the replacing imagery is not alive as the native inhabitants were. It is static. It can't dance. It can only do what it's told to do and what it sees to copy. It doesn't go out and see the world and make a contribution. It can't make you think and do things . . . and the ravished soul vacates. Absentee landlord.

Simultaneously the teacher takes over occupancy of the other houses in the street, the minds of the other children in his class, so that now we have the same kind of imagery in every one of the houses, all copies of the teacher, in a street named Conformity. As for all the former native occupants of the houses, now deceased, it's what I call murder of the imagery. Spiritually speaking, millions of children are murdered annually. Trained and paid to do it.

On the other hand, here is the enlightened skillful teacher strolling in the street, agog with interest in whom he meets, engaging in conversation. An interesting person at the least, so that people from the houses, the native inhabitants, are disposed to come out and meet him, exchange greetings and ideas with him. Sometimes with him and often without him, they feel free to think and do things . . . outside in the world. A street named Variation.

The teachers on the floor with the children at school are these strollers in the street. I know it but they don't know I know it. Nor do I tell them I know it, this being an untouchable, allergic to words. Time and privacy is what we want, as well as equipment and a jobs list. Very much we want these commodities . . . responsibility, equipment, privacy and time, but rapport is not lacking.

Though it's lacking with me. As I sit cross-legged on the floor with them to try a first lesson, I'm the first to know it. I've known it from the start, and the teachers have who have tried to help me with it. "When they get to know you," they say. "When you're more settled yourself."

But I've got to start sometime, and prepare my long cards and a black marker. "What word shall I write for you on this card?" I don't know his name. I'm still a stranger to the children so far who gravitate to the Americans.

"I dowanna word."

"Who are you?"

"Rocky."

"Yes, that's right, I remember," printing. "This word is Rocky."

"I don have to have a word," and gets up and goes.

Some little girls exquisitely dressed sit nearby. "I know your name," to one of them. "It's Odile. I'll write it for you on this."

"No," and turns from me. She passes for a girl but in truth she's a fairy, her dimensions from fantasy.

So I turn to another, all face and legs, wearing an outfit out of *Vogue*. "What is your name, then?"

"Durla."

"Of course. I remember." Having failed with the last

two names, I approach from another angle. "Whom do you love, Durla?"

"Nobody."

She does, but never mind. "I suppose you like someone. Like."

Two very pretty brown eyes survey the room and pause on a boy. "Gelo."

Now I can place Durla, the one who took two jobs. I print on the card, saying, "This is Gelo," but don't take her finger to trace it. She may not like the touch of me. Only ask diffidently, "What's this word?"

"Gelo," she concedes. Only warily she accepts the card but she examines the word "Gelo" with interest. Maybe it's a caption, I don't know; but she may have been holding the image of Gelo since school started. We'll see sometime later. Tomorrow, maybe. This is the time when she would write it, but . . . just but, that's all.

"Whom do you like, Bonnie?" I know she's four. Her eyes are soft pools of blue wonder and she mostly smiles on life.

"Jay," she replies of her friend beside her.

She watches while I print "Jay" on the card, and though I think she would not mind if I took her finger to trace it, I refrain(I don't touch or approach children unless they touch me first.) So far no one has, though I've just come from my grandchildren. The way things are going, they may never come to me at all. At least I can leave their fingers alone until they voluntarily touch me. Children are not common property just because they're small. I do, however, hold up the card, "What's this word?"

"Jay," and is pleased to take it.

But when I ask Jay herself for a word she wants, she squirms behind Bonnie and is silent. Afraid of the foreigner in me, no doubt, as many seem to be. Well, not exactly afraid but resistant. Resentful possibly of my British accent, or picking up contagiously my own unrest. Oh, many reasons. Dozens.

To a fierce little boy whom I remember, slim, dark and touchy, "And whom do you like, Peter?"

Pauses and turns, his dark eyes reflective. He has regular features, beautiful fingers. I get the feeling that half only of Peter's mind is on what is about him, the other half alertly on guard. One of these days, or some far day, I may be in the position to ask him what he is frightened of, but not now. Only, "Whom do you like, Peter?"

"Jonathon," he says, his gaze upon him.

I begin printing it but he's gone. And that's it. My first lesson on the K.V. here. The worst in my life. And so this is the way it's going to go: not from the inside out, from their loves at home, but through their friends at school. The word "love" makes them blush and they veer from it. Only two words, two names, is the score; Gelo and Jay. I'll hand the K.V. over to the Americans, who have been observing and with whom the children enjoy a natural rapport, until things are better between us. It is a rapport which creates a kind of order unrelated to authority.

"Do you think it's my accent, Carl?"

"No," reflectively. "They'll get used to having you round."

I'd like to remove those three pairs of small hands from that guitar before it and my sense of hearing are beyond repair, but since no one else minds, it must be all right and I'll have to learn to like it. Me learn to like discord? What about responsibility to the instrument? Freedom, I suppose. Never mind. Adapt and survive. Accept.

But it's terrible to so fail with the new eyes upon me of young teachers looking for a lead. Yet they're kindly to me and touch me with ease and don't seem to mind my accent. Eyebrows lift at my ways, though—this business about tea in the morning, and my recurring talk of order—but they're as indulgent to me as they are to the children, so that I recognize the snow in my heart.

Yellow the trees and still. They don't swing like those of home. And there's purple on the alien mountains and scarlet, as well as the wallowing yellow. I don't know how many days now since I left a plane for a school, for it's neither days nor weeks but years really pressed into pressured hours. I knew so much when I got off the plane and now I know nothing whatever, which in itself is the measure of time since I came; how far I've moved steadily backward instead of whirling forward.

Yet, excepting the hours at school, I'm radiantly happy here, wandering alone around strange corners and staring at the heights. True I'm lonely in the big yellow house alive with shadowy presences, but simultaneously glad of its size and height, being used to spaciousness and appreciative of the feel of silence.

Almost ceaselessly I think of the children at school and how to find form in my work, for shape and form is a need in work whatever your work is. When I was younger, I tussled for years over the place and the style of work. Which, for instance, was closer to God: love or work? And finally concluded . . . work. For love has seasons and can die in your hand, whereas work never falters. Work is the one acceptable replacement of memoried imagery. None need mourn if he can work.

When I first came, I was dreaming about stars in the firmament and of the many habitable planets light-years off, on one of which I'd see the spearpoint of civilization settling and inbreeding. But my thinking on education these days is a molten mass of questions only, spinning and whirling doubts as this Earth must have been before cooling and forming. Turbulence. Somewhere in the children the answers are, in a language yet to be decoded. Yet my thesis holds: whatever our child is, that's what his education is when you use his own imagery as working material; not wholly, but enough to keep it alive. Whether spearpoint or tail-end generation, his education cannot help suiting him; keeping pace, keeping in character with him. None of which excludes the handing down to him of the culture, whatever his culture is.

And so I think myself into a state of pacification on the subject of habitable planets. . . .

Yellow the trees and still. Golden the stars, and still too. Trees and stars make the story. How many centuries hence before some of us leave the trees for some arid planet like Mars? Tonight we may die, all over for us. We will not have been there among the stars.

Earth's course is run, its loins are able no more.
And its miserable children, thin, bald, and pallid
With pondering the everlasting problems too much.
Contemplate with empty eyes . . .

—JULES LAFORGUE

Here is the morning and here am I setting off early to school, to do preparation before the children come, which makes 7.30 a.m. Grossly uncivilized hour but accident supports it, as I choose early hours. I love to walk toward Mount Matin etched on the cold-blue sky, as impersonal and eternal as the moon himself as he surveys the Earth's problems. Walking to the spaceship poised for takeoff doing its preparation too: warming up its engines to overheat the cabins for overheated passengers. And what does this day hold? Never mind. Whatever Fate stirs in, whatever the spin, the gyration of the ship, it remains undeniably life. As I take out my key and open the hatch, the sun takes his key and opens the day.

I can't stand closed doors where children are segmenting the family fluidity, and when I see the door of the math room shut I take the liberty of opening it. I'm not one to intrude or invade if I can help it but, "That's no way for big boys to behave." Six and seven they are.

"We'll do what we like!" Crash the Cuisenaire rods on the floor.

"Standing on a table hurling things on the floor. That's like babies, not boys."

"We have every right to do what we like!" Bang, whiz, spin . . .

"Not like six and seven," I say. "You're both like little babies standing up there throwing valuable material that other children need. Babies."

"When you say something about someone," he shouts, "it sticks on yourself. It's you like the baby. You, you!" Crack, skid. "It's you that's the baby."

It's true. They're far cleverer than me. This is a modern open school and I've got to be that too. No pride or anything like that. No hurt. All being equal, he can say what he likes. And do what he likes too. I'm learning that reciprocal respect is not necessary to equality. On the other hand, am I respecting their right to release their imagery; who am I to criticize?

"It's you that's the baby," he repeats.

"Could be too. Me the baby. But in any case you bore me."

"And you bore us."

A jolly good answer. I'm floored again. Like the Cuisenaire rods. I try another way: "What makes you two think you're so clever?"

Flings more rods but he's thinking. "Because" . . . bash! . . . "we *are* clever."

"I agree. But does that make you interesting too?"

No answer from either.

"Why don't you answer?"

The bombs still pound the target but still there is no answer, so I walk toward the door, ashamed of victory.

"Yes, go," they say, "and shut the door. We want to be by ourselves."

I obey and shut the door. I'm getting the hang of equality and the evils of authority.

I stand in the tunnel-corridor while children run, collide and wrestle. What would the American teachers have done? I think I know. Without any debate, they might have got down on the floor, collected some rods as they landed and set about making a math pattern illustrating and honoring the function of the rods, so that in time the two might have joined them. But only might have. The rapport between American and American at work. But what did I do? Attacked.

I still stand while the children gambol. The corridor is lit by nylon lighting, the air by my standards overbreathed, overhot, reverberating from some tom-tom beat pulsing from a stereo. Too enclosing the architecture, built for thoughtful men rather than exploding children. Whose life am I living, mine or someone else's? Can't I stop the ship and get off?

I like children's voices, high, wild or low, solo or in unison, but the beat and the boom of stereo and the hitting of the suffering piano in the foyer . . . what is this thing, freedom, supplied to the children in overspilling glassfuls, in tankards, in brimming kegs? Must glorious freedom mean all this? Is this, indeed, freedom? If it is, what good is it? How long is the equipment going to last which they need for learning; the piano, the guitar, the Cuisenaire rods? And, as equipment, how long will I last? Astonishingly the Americans don't notice the noise; you can tell by their faces. They can talk and think along with it. Think and talk *better* along with it . . . with all the dire discords. Maybe they've made a mistake in summoning me, inviting an alien to them. Alien. There's the word. I should reel from it but I don't. I don't dislike being an alien. An artist must be an alien in life. Art must walk alone, a pariah of the human family.

But can't I get off? Where's a window? It's wide outside, the plain, within the cradling mountains. And still. What I need is a moment of seclusion or two to regroup my faculties. Adapt and survive . . . remember it.

Through the intoxicated children I weave my way, careful not to offend by touching, down the narrow spine of the ship to the storeroom, and plug in the pot for tea. This storeroom might be all trash cans, furnace, dirty mugs and pets, but it's where big things are said; where you meet everyone who is anyone, which includes guinea pigs and children. True there's no place for one to sit, but you get that kind of rest unrelated to chairs. Confidences are exchanged to the hum of the furnace, revelations to the smell of the trash cans; between teacher and teacher, child and child, between teacher and child; between parent and teacher, between parent and visitor, between everyone and everyone. Everything goes, from educational policy to exacting metaphysics and what happened at the last board meeting. In and out of season, the most important thing in life blossoms in this storeroom: that which passes between one and another, so that when Senta glides in to make some coffee I laugh and say, "My office."

A smile as she cleans a mug.

"I'm trying to work out what you mean by freedom."

"What I mean by freedom, or the kids, or the parents or the—?"

"Well, I mean . . . there's an intoxication . . . you know, it's not really what children are. It's . . . I don't want to use words like 'license' and 'anarchy,' but . . ."

"What happened was," from Senta, who is head of the upper school, "the kids were told before we opened they could do what they liked."

"We lost before we started, then."

"No, not quite," accurately, with a steady respect for facts, "but you can't start a school like this on immediate un-qualified freedom. Kids coming from structured schools should be given freedoms gradually. They should have brought the structure over to start with, then loosen up in stages. The kids are not used to it, not ready yet."

"Apparently."

And we laugh. "We can recover in time," quietly.

"Time. True. The main things we need are time and privacy. Who're all these people here every day? It's like an air terminal."

"Om . . . parents and visitors to see the school . . . there's great public interest you know, right? Crowds come every day wanting to teach. About nine volunteers walk in each morning. There's a big movement in the country, a breakaway from the traditional. There're thousands of these open schools."

I pour boiling water on the exposed tea leaves. If ever I'm asked to speak anywhere on education in this country, I'll lecture on how to make tea. "Senta. What you're telling me,

then, is that our children as they are now are not really normally as they are now. The frightening irresponsibility, the
. . ."

"Oh, no, no. No."

Meaning, I do not voice, that their contempt for me is no
more than a transitory symptom?

"The kids are all right," she assures. "When we get settled, when they . . ."

"At one stage yesterday, the infant room was packed
with grownups and there wasn't a child in sight."

"*C'est la révolution*," and we laugh again.

"Senta!" from a pretty girl child, throwing her arms
around her slim body, "Senta. I want you to come and see my
beadwork and tell me what to do next."

Now I'm talking to someone else. "Time and privacy is
all we want really," I repeat.

Conversation, however pointed, however critical, can't
last long in the thronged storeroom. Conversations can't last
long in the . . . conversations can't last . . . conversations can't . . . conversations . . .

Not unlike a cocktail party.

Carl is a young American whose rapport with the children is
as true as the hues on the mountains; no contrivance about it.
As casual as the heath at your feet. It is also, at this point,
indispensable. His outlook on life is the same as theirs, his
values, background and racial characteristics; his language
and even his legs, which he ties in a bow beneath him. That
he's also an anthropological graduate I know by accident
only.

As a man rolls up his sleeves to a job, Carl takes off his

socks to a job, so that his feet are what you notice. There's rarely no smile mixed up with his glasses somewhere inside his whiskers, and our children use him as a commodity, an item of equipment they don't have to put away. As I do too. You seldom see how tall he is, he usually being cross-legged on the floor. Although standing, he swings high like a cotton-wood; in ego he swings low like the sage. Self-effacingly.

You can climb all over him if you like, over his back, knees and head, as you can climb all over his mind . . . through, under or behind it. You can crawl right through his smile to the storeroom of his knowledge, finger what's there and help yourself to it whether you put things back or not.

Getting the children to do their jobs is climbing a mountain backward. "We need some children to help the teachers," I say, "to see that everyone does his job. A couple of policemen to . . ."

Outrage from the teachers. "You can't do that!"

"Oh?"

"D'you know what that means, Mrs. H.?"

"Policemen?"

"That means pigs in this country."

"Pigs? It means friends in our country."

Carl reproves, "You can't use that word, Mrs. H."

"Heavens. What'll we use, then?"

"Not *pigs*!" Horror.

"Helpers, then?"

"But we're *all* helpers."

I've no doubt you are, I do not say, but in a way not immediately obvious. "Friends . . . can we use that?"

"We're *all* friends."

"I take it," warming up, "that what you're all telling me is that no one is in the position to ask the children, *expect* the children, to help us with the other children?"

Doggedly, "They don't like any one of them to be in authority over any other."

"They 'don't like.' Interesting." The authority terror again. No wonder they go in for the wannadowanna. I'm baffled. I don't know what to do about the terror of authority. New ground. New country to colonize. In some societies, the police are as close to the people as bartenders and butchers. I sit a moment on the floor to think it over while our children careen, carouse and climb. I'm recalling other children I've known honored to be the policemen, and children who like being policed by each other. If we could get clear of politics, we could get on with teaching. Where the devil has the *substance* of education got to? Ah! I've got it. "Have you got anything against the word 'captains'?"

No one answers at once. No one stops Rocky from standing on the guitar while Monty unscrews the strings.

"You do have captains in this country, don't you . . . in sport?"

Carefully thoughtful, examining it.

"Aren't I allowed to ask a boy to bring in the children, for instance? After all, he's more agile and energetic than I am. I can be preparing their work. I can do things that he can't and he can do things that I can't. Or does it work only one way in an open school—in an open country, if you like: that I do things that he can't but he's too free to do things that I can't? Is this what you mean by equality?" How holy is this equality?

No one answers. I find American graduates most careful about their thinking, sacrificing all for it like a woman in love. I know that when an answer does come it won't be irresponsible.

"Is that guitar of any value to anybody? We've already lost the use of the ukulele."

A soft voice says to Rocky, "Would you like to put the guitar on the table?"

Or would you *not* like? I keep to myself.

"I dowanna."

Another voice says, still soft, "Captains. That's all right."

I may be wrong. Everyone here thinks better than I do with my passion and metaphor. Maybe it's authority to bring in the children at all. Maybe we should sit talking, waiting for some whim to move the children to come inside. A test of our TV entertainment value to lure them in. How can you teach anyone anything at all when all, irrespective of age, knowledge or experience, are exactly equal? Since democracy is based on envy, presumably equality is too. Whereas I'm here to teach, rather than serve or baby-sit.

The teachers carefully agree to the word "captains" and, having had enough of this will-you-won't-you, will-you-won't-you, will-you-join-the-dance, I choose the captains myself, dammit. I choose three boys who hang together whose leader has a certain charisma. Boys who seem to me interesting people, more bored than the rest, being not extended, more mature. The boys indeed who were throwing the rods with only contempt for me. Zed of seven, leaning in doorways, whose vivid, livid imagination ensures arduous followers . . . Agar and Henry. Zed Zane & Co. Boys who live their lives more in the mind than with hands and legs and who have personal drawing power. It's true that Henry hurts me when he sticks out his tongue and calls me dum-dum, but I realize I am a dum-dum. I've never heard the word before, but its meaning gets through. Who knows? I may soon be American.

"This meeting is too long," states Henry.

"I hate meetings," from Jonathon.

"I hate the word itself."

"Can we go to snack now?"

"Those who don't work don't eat. Those who work . . . do. Please yourselves whether you do your jobs or not. But those who have, come and sit by me," cross-legged on the floor. And, I might mention, within the door.

Authority, Equality, Freedom. Yet someone did use the word "Responsible" one day. Oh, yes, it was Carl: each is responsible for his own possessions. Not: each is responsible for all possessions, which is too collective. It makes some sense on paper, but there's far too much paper anyway, with or without sense on it. Take all the paper from North America, and the country would come right in a week. And another thing: as child after child comes and sits before me, his work done behind him, and I lay a hand on his head . . . Another thing: what in God's name do they mean by teaching? What in Freedom's name, I should say. Adapt and survive or go home.

But it is sweet, oh, so sweet! . . . the little ones sitting before me. So sweet to lay a hand on each head. "This one is here," I murmur. "This one, this one, this one. And here is this one, and this one, and good heavens here is this one. *Now* you can go to snack."

I don't think Earth's course is run, her loins no more able;
nor is my own course run. True I'm not yet equal to the K.V.
with the children, for one reason and another . . . rapport-
lessness mainly, confidencelessness minorly . . . but others
are. Any of the American teachers are. My intellectual loins
are sufficiently able to delegate this. Carl takes over the K.V.,
and in a few days there are several words from several of the
children. Durla has "Gelo," which she still recognizes,
"baby" and "Manly," the baby at home; Bonnie has "Jay,"
her school friend, "Daddy" and "Odile"; the wide-eyed Peter
with the dimple and the delicate fingers has "Jonathon," his
current interest, "Peter," "car" and "Michael," though I
don't know who Michael is; Rocky asks for "Janice" (his
mother) and "fun house," and other children who have

frankly rejected me release imagery to Carl. Praise God for American teachers round. The fairy Odile, who'd refused me even her own name, tells Carl three male names in a row: "Waring" (surname), "Bob" (father's name) and "Harry" (brother), which is just about the natural beginning, while even the shy, resisting Jay has asked for "Grandma Ann." So nothing is lost. They ask for names, every one of them, though mostly names of other children. "Doesn't anyone ask for his own name yet?"

"No."

"Hasn't anyone asked for 'Mommy' and 'Daddy' yet?"

"Odile's names are her family, and Rocky's name is his mother. Bonnie," fingering the cards, "is the only one who has actually used the word 'Daddy.' "

"But only between the names of her friends, Jay and Odile."

"And Jay has asked for 'Grandma Ann.' "

"Which is near home," I add. "Quite a cheering score, really. From the inside, I mean," taking the cards. "All Odile needs is the name of her mother and here is a happy child." No doubt all of them are normal; it's only the evidence lacking. "How interesting it will be to see Odile's next word."

Another week with Carl, and Jonathon has started off getting the idea. "Stuck" is his first word, "helicopter" next, then "blood" and "wood." Not names this time. Monty starts off with "house," withdrawn the next day since he doesn't know it, then asks for "Daddy," "the East," then "house" again, which he does know next day this time. House means something much to him. Gelo begins with "bike"—he has a new one—"Peter," who interests him, then stalls and takes off outside on the plain to play on the big rock, where in no time he is joined by followers. There are still children who don't start at all, and no one presses them.

All very nice, all well enough, considering the gyrating of the ship, but where is the movement from the inside out I'm accustomed to see? But for two or three, where is the inside anyway? Awkward to have one like me around. Exploring on a Sunday, I think it out or try to think it out. There's one thing sure: it cannot be the absence of rapport between me and our children, for there's plenty of that with Carl. Nor my accent and being an alien, for there're three American teachers on the floor actively with them. Of course, it could well be that many of them have already passed the inside-outside sequence at home and are already at the outside interests.

If not, then it could be their agitation at the beginning of a new kind of school, new teachers, new ways, new freedoms; intoxication at the heady drinks of freedom to which they are not accustomed at school, the impact of the care and concern of the teachers to which some . . . and the attention of the teachers . . . which some may not know at home, given the new kinds of homes these days, and the desired man-presence accessible to them . . . in Carl. Anything that's new and sudden unsettling them.

Or it could be the agitation of the race itself of which Americans tell me, revealing itself in the K.V. of its newest generation, but that may be taking it too far. But the thought which arrests me most is the one about their being like this anyway: the third dimension of their imagery sedated or even extinguished, bombarded out of action by overstimulation, the feeling stilled. The house of the mind gate-crashed and occupied by invading nonliving imagery. If so, I might as well go home. And they too. Is the new generation of any post-industrial, swiftly evolving society to end up two-dimensional only, a kind of space society; a spearpoint to take off one day to some far habitable planet? Actually? Too far-fetched. Fiction. But so was landing on the moon fiction once.

Multiplying questions. I'll have the chance of answering them some desired day when our children and I accept each other. Desired day . . .

Tentatively I try the K.V. again. Much of my reluctance is now sheer straight-out shyness before the teachers in front of whom I failed the first time. Not because they're teachers, not from any lack of indulgence from them or understanding . . . they're as good to me as they are to the children . . . but because I failed before. You're nervous if you're not sure of your work, a fact I learnt long ago when performing on the piano. If you're sure of it, you're all right; if you're not sure . . . you're not.

Will anyone accept me yet? Cross-legged on the floor among them, I find that Rocky does, who asks for "Frank." Gelo asks for "Mrs. Henderson" . . . astonishing! And when blue-eyed Bonnie edges near enough I ask her outright, seeking important imagery, "Whom do you love best in the world, Bonnie?"

"Mommy," which I write. The first time the word has surfaced so far from anyone at all. A word outdated.

But when I ask Peter the same question he only replies, "Jonathon," as he did the other day. Which brings up a provocative point about Jonathon: he's a boy concerned with personal relationships with other boys. But of course, one ar-

56

gues. What I mean is that he's normally concerned with his boy playmates, whereas I sometimes find this missing here. You hear on Jonathon's tongue the words "best friend," and you see him dejected if rejected. I've seen him begging Henry, "Will you be my best friend, my very best friend?" and being rejected because Henry follows Zed Zane. The attachments and rejections do happen among small children, as well as among the older. I've seen them under way at three: two little faces kissing between a crack in the back fence. And here's young Peter, with romance in his eyes . . . his first word "Jonathon." The second one too. Warmth begets warmth, engenders it, and Peter contagiously catches Jonathon's warmth. I'd rather Peter's first and second words were from home, however, but you can only take what comes.

Not that you see Peter and Jonathon playing together. Jonathon is attracted by Henry, who is attracted by Zed Zane. But Peter is not bereft. He lives the whole thing which he wants in his mind, behind his glowing eyes, preferring this way to reality. There's a great and deep story behind Peter's word asked two days running: "Jonathon," from which inadvertently, as well as deliberately, he learns to read and write.

It's the use of this image of Peter's which is vital: the picture in mind of Jonathon, his admiration for and his wishes concerning him in some impossible dream. The *exercise* of this imagery, which is an indispensable organ of his mind, by the *use* of it. This image of Jonathon doesn't run to hide beneath the stairs to die of deprivation, but lives on strongly in the house of his mind; from his eyes his soul in a look. And as he writes in forming each letter, each strange shape he makes takes on his passion in its contour. Writing it means Jonathon to him, reading it means Jonathon. Reading and writing are glorified, taking on interest forever.

Yes, and others respond a little. Henry's first words are "my birthday," Candy's first word is "Beverly." Candy is small, vital, vivacious, who says just what she thinks, what she feels, and she feels a lot . . . anything that surfaces. There's no holdup of Candy's imagery into her throat and over her tongue. Her tongue can deal with anything that comes. Someone you soon get to know, Candy.

"Is Beverly your mother?" I risk. I haven't been engaging our children in conversation as I like to do in order to exercise their imagery, feeling that it might be felt by them as an affront from an alien. When I know them better I will, and they know me better. But something in Candy invites me to risk it.

"I didn say she's my mother. How come you keep saying she's my mother?"

"Why do you keep on saying that I say Beverly's your mother when I don't?"

"Okay, okay, you don't. But she isn my mother, right?"

"I've got it. Beverly isn't your mother."

"You catch on, huh?"

"Catch on what?"

Thrusts forward her small face to mine, her blue eyes blazing. "Don't you unnerstand *anything*!"

"Depends on what country I'm in."

She likes this answer, though only five. Relaxes and looks me over. "A-huh," whatever this means.

"Candy. I've got the message that Beverly's not your mother. Your sister, I suppose."

58

"She's not my sister. How come you don't know my sister's in Florida?"

"How should I? No one told me."

Her face near mine, "You have to be told *everything*, right?"

"Just about, in this country. So Beverly's not your mother, not your sister. She must be a friend of yours."

Flings her hands in despair. "She's not my friend, she's not!"

Some might call this converse but . . . "Is she your enemy, then?"

"She's not my enemy," resigned. "Right?"

"Wrong."

Pause. Her little white teeth grip together. "Can you *hear*?"

"Can you *explain*?"

"Beverly's my doll."

"Well, why didn't you . . . never mind." Hold up the card. "What's this word?"

"Don't you know *yet*?" and storms off to the clay room to make wild shapes.

Learn and survive . . . right?

Along with other not-done-yets, the adaptation of the use of the formula "Release the native imagery of our child and use it for working material." It calls on all I've seen of cultures in other countries on this Earth whose course is run, its loins able no more. Once my marrow is scattered, my course will be run too, so that one looks at everything left in it, and every people too; even that Thrice-Great Magician, the Devil, cradled in evil and rocking our souls.

None of what I've seen is for these children, the advance

guard of technology, with their long legs, proud faces and elongated bodies, the thrice-great brains; least of all for these their own traditional education. Yet as I walk near the river, wandering and wondering, as I think, as I consider the imagery behind my own eyes, I do remind myself that I have lived but a few weeks within these mountains close to the moon and that what I wonder as I wander could be something less than accurate. Like visitors to my own country letting fly in the press. So that instead of assuming, This is such, That is so, it's better to hold your horses. In the company of the trees where the waters watch, I do hold these horses, thinking, This *may* be so and yet may not.

For what I'm so warily considering is whether education in North America is or is not three decades behind the people herein, so fast have I found the society evolving in the little ones. A people can outstrip its own education and its vocabulary also. Education needs at least to keep up with the people it serves—never mind with other countries—and its vocabulary as well.

Swift overtumbling evolution calls for as swift and overtumbling a manner of education; a flexible mobile accompaniment that can twist and probe, spring and somersault to keep abreast of our children themselves. A vocabulary made of elastic, of sensitive rubber, changing form as variously as water. The sciences keep their vocabularies abreast of themselves, so why not education?

The only form of education I know which automatically renews with a people is the oldest. Only the oldest man can teach the newest. When the working material is supplied by our children, it changes with our children. Our education drawn from the native imagery, whatever it happens to be, fits him as well as the organs of his body; the first grunting man the teacher. Sever the new man from the old and you cut continuity, and in losing continuity we lose a dimension indispensable to wholeness. Only organic education can halt man from becoming inorganic. Three dimensions we need for man on Earth; two will do for the moon.

None of which, as I've remarked, is to discountenance, disregard, discredit the handing down of the culture also when we encounter new ideas not arisen in ourselves: reading books we have not written ourselves, seeing things we would not otherwise have seen . . . whatever the condition of whatever the culture for, just as the organic education keeps abreast of us, so do we keep abreast with the culture.

Of course our Earth has run its course if it rots where the seeds are. Of course its loins are no longer able if they rot at the genitals. But after all, why not? Let the spearpoint take off to that habitable planet I hear of in the galaxy . . . it's got the brains to do it. And let the tail end return to nature . . . it's got the heart to do it.

After which pallid pondering I go home and make the tea, then play some human Schubert.

None of which is to say, my dear North Americans . . . and if my affection is something out-of-date it is because my imagery remains intact . . . none of which is to . . . because I never saw anything you could call a book until I was eleven and that was a prize I won, the *Legends of Greece and Rome*; no unskilled teacher invaded the privacy of the house of my mind and took over occupancy; my imagery danced, fought, ate and lived and exercised itself . . . none of which is to say that we suddenly sweep away all the old education and plonk on the new, bang! No. The education of the future needs the education of the past as new leaves need the tree. Only the deadwood of the lower boughs needs to come off with a chain saw so the new leaves can come away. We don't cut down the tree; we need the trunk and the roots bred from history. The new leaves need the nutriment from the soil in the sap from the past.

In the old education there is much that's retainable, as we all know. I'm not speaking of this country alone at the moment. I sit in the desks with our children in the most formal of classrooms, doing what they do from the BB, listen as they do, and there are teachers I'd like to take back with me to an open school . . . or not. There are teachers I like to come back to where they are. Energy and curiosity make good desk mates.

No, we don't cut down the tree. Education needs its yesterdays.

When I wake in the morning, it is snowing again . . . I hadn't known it. I've been awake during the night but hadn't heard. When I get up and look outside to see what sort of day . . . strange! The scape is white.

The hour is alive with floating flakes, the new morning full of them. They have no sound as they fly on every whimful current, as they flip inconsequently. You can see wherever the air is breathing by the spinning of the flakes. Often colliding, the careless flakes, to fall regretfully.

What I love about the snow, it is so soft . . . to touch and be touched by. When I walk abroad or alone uptown, it decorates my coat or my hair maybe, and kisses my face sympathetically.

It does not hit you like the rain or sudden memory and it

doesn't soak like tears; doesn't push like the wind of circumstance or pull demandingly. It lets you walk in peace.

Its coldness warms this other cold in the place where I kept my heart. The outer snow melts the inner snow in the place where I kept my love; its purity informs me. This is what's strange about the snow: its coldness thaws and warms me.

In the universal order . . . frail, unique human marvel.

—JULES LAFORGUE

Odile is usually to be found with Candy . . . she fairy, Candy fire. Odile, having given Carl three male family names, agrees to confer with me, changes course and asks for "Janet." Now if only this Janet were her mother, we'd have the classic example. I do not assume it and dare not ask, just lightly play round it. "Is Janet your friend?"

"No," mischief.

"I know who she is; your sister."

"I don't have a sister." Candy likes the game too.

"Not your friend, not your sister; your doll, maybe?"

"A-a."

"What does that mean; yes or no?"

"No."

But sometimes it means yes. How am I to know?

"A-a is yes. A-a is no."

"I still can't tell the difference."

"A-a . . . that's yes."

"A-a," I repeat.

"A-a . . . that's no."

"A-a." I seem to be grunting like primitive man. I do hear that many are seeking the primitive life. The vocabulary moving backward.

"You don't say it right." She laughs. "A-a, a-a."

"You're teasing me."

"A-a," with a nod of the head.

"Yes or no?"

"No," laughing outright. "You can't learn it, Mrs. H."

"Kahore."

She's puzzled but doesn't ask, "What's that?" They don't ask questions here, which is one of my ponderings when wandering on Sunday. You can see she is wondering what it means, but you don't ask questions of the TV screen. With no revision, recapitulation or questions, it flashes on to the next. Take it or leave it or turn off the knob. Shall I tell her? She could go on wondering forever. "Kahore. The Maori for no."

She doesn't repeat it; I'm a TV screen, entertaining rather than teaching.

"Can you say it? Kahore?"

"Kahore," laughing, wriggling. Quite possibly she's wondering about the Maori for yes, or is the curiosity of this generation sedated? Another Don't Know piles on the others.

"Now where in heaven were we?"

"Not my friend, not my sister, not my doll."

"Who is Janet?"

"My mother." Her mother. That makes the whole family. Odile is the rule that proves the exceptions.

Milly whispers "baby" to me, which is dead-center home. There's a flush of joy and pride on her sweet thoughtful face, which is what I mean by native imagery. The word "baby" spoken with feeling is a caption of a genuine complete home, man-woman love enchanting it and several brothers and sisters along with the baby. I show her the card: "baby."

A few more consent to confer with me, with or without rapport, and I don't get too much cheek. Maybe they're getting used to having me round, as Carl remarked; accent, alien and all.

I never miss walking alone on Sunday with the snow falling. My stick I've found in the big yellow house lent for my occupation. It has carving at the top and a tuft of feathers, and they say, "Where did that come from?" They say other things when I appear uptown with my stick, my bag and snowboots, like, "Hi! How're ya doin?"

I simply love to walk abroad in the snow, and the more it is snowing the better. A friend wrote in a letter from home, "When people first meet the snow, they have this tremendous personal reaction." To feel it on my face and to see the limitless whiteness is something catalytic. Some fairy tale of childhood has plainly come true and I simply have to believe it, whereas it cannot be true.

I see no authority in the town, none poised above another. An easy interflowing of everyone; inter-respect and inter-trust. I suppose someone does tell someone else to do

something and I suppose staff gets fired for being too easy—
there must be authority somewhere—but the overall view is
utopian.

What does the school hate so much about this word
"authority"? I don't mind authority myself when I know it is
informed and fair. I miss very much a headmaster at school
to go to for directions, someone accomplished in the mechan-
ics and nuances of running a school, knowing the techniques
in a classroom also, the interplay among teachers. I look for
all this every day. As it happens, Life is authority, the headmaster of a global school. I found that out as early as my
teens . . . if not earlier. Life says, "Obey my laws or
perish." He says, "Take what you want from me but pay for
it." He pronounces, "Now there will be winter."

No, no, I don't want winter!

But there will still be winter. The seasons are part of my
rhythm.

Who are you to impose your seasons on me!

Save your breath, mortal, and I'll save mine. It's below
zero today so put on warm clothes.

No, no, I dowanna!

Then perish, wretch.

I dowanna perish!

Too bad.

I wanna be free an do what I like. I want freedom!

Then pay for it.

How much?

You pay in the coin of responsibility.

I don like responsibility. I dowanna pay!

In that case, you don't get freedom. You get something
very much cheaper, of little value: license, anarchy.

No, it is freedom. I know best. I don have to pay for anythin. I jus take it!

Do. But perish.

I won't perish!

Carry on and find out for yourself. I don't build myself entirely round what you wanna or dowanna and never mind the rest. There are two laws, man's and mine. The man-made wannadowanna and mine: obey or perish. Please yourself.

> May there be nothing known
> Of this rotten Brain which was the Earth, one day!

Well, try another planet.

"It's time now, little ones, to . . . sorry. It's time now, big ones, to pick up our things and put them away. Time to do our jobs."

"I dowanna," from Rocky.

"If we don't care for our things, Rocky, there'll be no things left to care for."

Sudden inspiration, his blue eyes alight with vision, seeing some alternative to responsibility: the senior school, maybe, where the big boys are engaged in marvelous science; the snack banquet in the foyer and the encounters in the hall with . . . oh, anything but see to his things. A marvelous idea. "I wanna go."

"But what about your things?" Glance at board. "You're the blackboards boy, with Agar."

A reflective somersault on the floor. "I'll put them away tomorrow."

Angela from Grade 2 has a feeling of responsibility—

built in, I think. Maybe assimilated from her mother. She's seven. Her face would shame any angel and her fair curls swinging to the waist would bring a big price in a wig shop. Reprovingly to Rocky, "That's what you said yesterday, Rocky, but you didn't. Your things were lost today."

Rocky has a brain too like the rest and, like them, is lovely to look at; clear round blue eyes, snow skin and pale blond hair cut low on his brow. Most of our children are fair like angels, as a Roman Emperor remarked of the Anglo-Saxons brought back as slaves to Rome. "Not Angles," he mused, "but Angels." Rocky leans near the window observing the falling snow until suddenly a conclusion arrives in his eyes; not willfulness but conviction. A great idea. "I dowanna." The solution to all.

Angela debates better than I ever will. "But, Rocky, if you don't have your books and pencils and blackboards and stuff, that means you can't learn anything, right?"

The new and great idea gathers in size and wonder as his eyes widen. "I dowanna learn."

He could be right. He's a poet.

Durla of five joins in. "I wanna learn. I wanna put away my things and stuff and do my jobs. I wanna learn." She comes from an academic family.

"Rocky," I say. Poet, inspiration or not. "Your blackboards are going to be put away before you go to snack, and packed neatly in the corner. No work, no snack." What would I do without Life behind me? "Those who don't work don't eat."

"I'm gonna eat."

Angela takes over. "If you don't do your share, who is?"

"Not me."

"He must have brought his servants to school," I remark. "Has anyone seen them around; a whole row of tall men in livery like the king had in the story."

"I don have any servants to bring."

"Too bad. Tell me, what are you, Rocky?"

"A boy."

"Who are all these?"

"Kids."

"As long as you don't mistake them for servants in livery; yours." A memory surfaces of my own sons and this very situation. And of what I said to them at the time; "You know what, Rocky? What you want is a wife," which is far from fair. I regret it. Not fair to wives as well.

"I'm sick of this!" striding round and shouting like a man come home drunk to his family. "I wanna go. I wan my snack. I have every right to have my snack. I don care about the blackboards. I dowanna put em away. I-I," voice rising, "I dowanna learn!"

"Why come to school, then?" from Angela. "Howcome you don't stay home?"

"I dowanna stay home. I wanna come to school."

Want will be your master, I do not say. I'd been infuriated when my sister said it. But I drop the subject, keeping the other children waiting. "All right, little . . . big ones, I mean, when all your jobs are done: pencils picked up, counted, and in the box, books stacked neatly on the table, blocks in their right boxes, chalk in the tin, what else? Blackboards in the corner . . ." I'm sitting on the floor with them because I like it. "When the art room is tidy and the brushes done, the clay in the clay room covered with a wet cloth . . .

let me see. The Cuisenaire rods and puzzles in the math room . . . who are the paper people? When everything is off this floor and in its place . . . then we'll go to snack."

Angela says, "The Grade 2 room is all done."

"Good. The Grade 2 children can go."

Jonathon wails, "I want my snack."

"Are your blocks done?"

"Yeah."

"Sit by me, Jonathon," and touch his head. "This one has done his work, this one, this one," touching their heads, "this one," as the Maoris say, "this one and this one." In spite of all of which, Gerald still holds an escape idea. "I wanna call my Mommy," successfully raising two large gray silky tears that would break the heart of the Devil himself, that Thrice-Great Magician. But not the austere heart of the authority . . . Life.

Two things come to me as I sit cross-legged on the floor and they collect before me, most of us ready now. Even Rocky has been swept up in the current of collective energy of what everyone else is doing. One is that men often do find it sheer agony to clean up after themselves, my own sons included, not to mention my grandsons. And the other . . . but I've forgotten.

At least this is a law of life: those who don't work don't eat. Obviously many of us who don't work do eat, including the doctor in Chekhov's play; some of us are nature's observers, umpires keeping the score. Even so, they are keeping the score. But in time we collide with some other of life's laws: the one about boredom, for instance. Absence of occupation is no rest; a mind quite vacant is a mind distressed, being those of us who do not even keep the score. Whereas boredom, to be bored, is the second sin in my reckoning. Not to mention the first agony as in Chekhov's *Three Sisters*. We who don't work don't eat, and we who don't eat don't live. And to live is the idea, I take it.

Oh, yes, I remember that other thing now: the collective energy in a group of children, an electric current; at its worst mob rule, at its best sympathy. At times an irresistible fashion, a contagion of feeling gathering up most little people to do what all are doing. Unwittingly they become one personality, even the Rockys, Geralds and Jonathons, each an ingredient, a proportion of the whole. A common current running through them, so that when you've achieved a routine you can dispense with individual confrontations like these, have no occasion to engage disciplines, Life's or Man's. The thing just runs regardless.

For, contrary to what appears to be, routine has a rhythm and a rhyme to it which answers man's immortal need for monotony and symmetry, as well as for surprise. Work is not all inspiration. There can be vanity and danger in inspiration alone.

"Not that I mind it, Carl, all these people coming, staying, talking, going, but . . . I like people and gaiety, but . . ."

He's on the floor with one or two children. So am I. Who is this leaning against me? Peter, of all people. "There's great public interest in this school, Mrs. H., and the parents are involved. They made it, right?"

Perhaps I should answer A-a, or is yes A-a?

"Right?" he repeats.

Much beauty in the parents: eyes, teeth, voices, legs, an inbreeding of physical beauty, right? In the way we breed stud horses in our country, wrong? "It's all new to me. Lovely but new. I've simply never seen parents so engaged with a school before."

"They want to see what they've made."

"I can see them doing some teaching in time, when we've got hold of the thing—when we get a chance to get hold of the thing, I mean. An endless supply of staff. They can hand down the culture in the afternoons. Marvelous."

Carl ruminates from behind a child's head. "That's why they come. They're an interested part in what they've made and in what they've paid for."

"What about the dogs?"

"We're all very fond of dogs."

"They behave just like people," I note, "and are treated as people. Well, let's give the dogs their K.V. too, since I can't find enough children."

"There're quite a few children up there."

"Who's going to catch them? Where are our captains?"

Carl collects about twelve, a good score out of nearly thirty, under the circumstances. "There's only one thing," I say to him, "routine. So they know what to do, feel where to go, relax in a shape around them. It's a protection and a haven for them from their bewilderment—from what they think is freedom, if you like. This doesn't happen to be freedom as it is; it's intoxication. They're only children, and need direction finders. Routine, shape, stability. Where are those other boys?"

"Out on the plain. That big rock draws them like a magnet."

Cards, black marker. Bonnie speaks "ring," from one on her finger, Peter says "junk," Candy proclaims her surname, "Rivers Bell," a word from home, and I take a third thought on Candy. Plainly her third dimension operates still. Milly again has a word from home, "doll," and I think the same of her. Interestingly, it's these children with normal vocabularies who are ready to learn . . . work that out. Odile is here with "King," her dog, all of whose words so far have been sincere key vocabulary, all from the securities and loves of home to which she has easy access.

Shy Jay asks me for "hopper," which turns out to be some kind of insect under the house which has impressed her, frightened her maybe—a grasshopper, I'd say.

The next sequence is to write these words, but they don't seem to favor handwriting. There are acres of paper and forests of pencils, but it will be better when they accustom themselves to using the small blackboards and chalk and dusters. You could drown in the paper and be lost without trace.

Recess and snack, a banquet midmorning in the foyer; then, "What about putting on your coats and boots and running outside in the snow?"

"Dowanna." Finish.

I settle down at the two-foot square referred to as the table, open a slit of window on the snow and turn to recording on my large folded card the words they have so far given us. To Carl, Durla has given the name of another girl, "Gemmy," Jonathon has "chalk-peeler," Monty's first word is "house," Gerald's first word is "Daddy" and Jennifer's is "flower." I examine all the words on the folder to date, trying to read some pattern or order. Let me see, now, thirteen children . . . but the outside door, two feet from me, swings constantly as senior children exercise their *every right* to burst in and out of my room, which has to be an authorized highway. Authorized, did I say? Steady on that word. But children do have to burst in and out of something, myself included. We're right.

Thirteen children of the twenty-two in the K V movement. No, I count again, fourteen.

ROCKY: *Janice* (mother), *fun house, car, Frank.*
GELO: *bike, Peter, Mrs. Henderson.*
BONNIE: *Jay, Daddy, Odile, Mommy, ring.*
DURLA: *Gelo, baby, Manly* (baby's name), *Gemmy.*
JAY: *Grandma Ann, hopper.*
PETER: *Jonathan, Peter, car, Michael, Jonathon, junk.*
CANDY: *Beverly, Rivers Bell.*
MONTY: *house, Daddy, the East, house.*
GERALD: *Daddy.*
MILLY: *baby, doll.*
ODILE: *Waring, Bob, Harry, Janet* (all home names), *King* (dog).
JONATHON: *stuck, helicopter, blood, wood, chalk-peeler.*
HENRY: *my birthday.*
JENNIFER: *flower.*

Not too bad, really. Five out of these fourteen have started off with a home word; Rocky, Jay, Gerald, Milly, Odile. But how many have the normal pattern of the outward flow? Odile only so far. One out of fourteen. What about the other thirteen: who are they, where are they? What are they here for, what am I here for?

By God, it's after eleven. Time we were well under way with the Intake. Shouldn't be hard to bring along, since they didn't go outside. "Come, little ones," from past ways.

"I'm just going outside," says one.

"Howcome you call us jus when we're going outside?" another.

"Come, Rocky," hand on shoulder. "Come into school."

Squirms from me. "I dowanna."

"Monty, come in now. We'll have our reading."

"I don have to read. I'm going outside."

"We're all going to do our reading now."

"I don have to."

I cruise up the hall among the erupting life, the voices, running, squealing, wrestling and the exploding excitement. I'm recruiting. "Come into school, Durla. Odile? Jonathon? Come, we'll do our reading. Gelo? Peter? Come into school. It's time to come into school."

A few do. Durla and Odile. Perhaps in this foreign context, I should not have called them, which could be said to be pressure, compulsion. *Force* is the word. Force. Now Carl appears, all of him, winding his way through the multitude from the office, with Jacky on his back, and some of the little ones run to him in little less than radiance, taking his hand. "Would you like," he says, smiling, "to come into meeting now?"

Would you like. Ah. I erred. I'd said, "Come into school."

With Carl they are quiet and attentive in no time, he leading with a clapping action on his knees, they imitating. He stops, they stop and all are quiet, so that he speaks to them softly and reasonably as to adult friends about coming into meeting when they are called. And they listen and answer like adults, reasonably, ably, articulately. It's equality, the real thing. I address them as young children, which is not equality. Now how can I learn to . . . how can I stop addressing young children as young children? Perhaps they are not young children at all and that's where my error is. Perhaps they *are* grown-up. Maybe they never knew real child-

hood. But as an argument this is far-fetched. I'm more a
child than they are.

They would be reading now in groups of two or more
the words of their own they've accumulated, talking about
them, teaching each other knee to knee, hearing each other,
spelling them, associatively discursive, but when this is
begun—their admirable attention to Carl when he was talking to them; entertaining them, really—it fragments into personal and physical interchanges, as indeed I mean it to be,
except that words are forgotten amid gamboling and rolling
and an occasional somersault, every man for himself. I mean
the personal interchange through the words, the relationships, the embraces and antagonisms, the laughter blending
with recriminations and dark whispered secrets but stem-
ming from their words. Their words do not seem to be part of
them. All very pretty to look at, of course, and romantic.
From where I am on the floor among them, I could sit here
myself among their voices for the rest of the morning, for
what's left of the morning, myself wallowing in the wannadowanna; I could. But where is the learning they come for?
Even Carl can't get them to cooperate with one another . . .
cooperation, that's what's missing, the desire to *do*, to help
one another. Carl decides to read them a story instead and
quickly they group in T.V. attention, clustering round him
like chickens—or like children, rather—while the teacher en-
tertains.

When the story is over, the lunch banquet again spread
on the canvas in the foyer, after which a few go out and play
in the snow, two or three boys. Agree to go out. Then the
careering, careening up the hall again, the long, carpeted,
hot, overbreathed length of it made for children to romp in, to

rollick in. I would myself. It's gay. Some knocked over by bigger ones, though, collisions, so that amid squeals of delight you hear sudden crying. Peter is stamping his feet up and down the keyboard until I lift him down. No one else does. It's freedom. "You don't put your feet on a keyboard, only your fingers. Feet hurt a piano. Hear him crying?"

He resists willfully as he must, for I am bigger than he is. What do the staff and children think of me now, using *Force* on a boy? A five-letter word. Peter swings round to hammer the keys again with his fists, and Henry joins him on principle, their small faces lifted to me in defiance. Yet Peter is the boy who leaned on me half a day ago. Henry spits, "You dum-dum!" and on they go.

The stereo is flat out also, filling the ship, cramming it from bow to stern, together with the ghastly discord from the piano. The children's voices yes, give me children's voices which have always sounded like water to me, but . . . one of the staff is discussing with me some fine point of . . . of what? I don't know. How can people stand this uproar from the piano, the discord? How can anyone stand discord? "I don't know what you're saying."

"Why?"

"This . . . this stereo. The . . . I can't think with all that on. I can't teach with it."

"The stereo? Is it on?"

"Don't you hear it?"

"Oh, that. It's like that all over America, Mrs. H."

"You mean . . . you Americans can think with all that on?"

"We don't hear it."

"Do you hear the piano? The discord?"

"That's a strong piano. It can take it."

But can ears take it? I say only, "I'm used to silence when I'm thinking. I can't think at all with that competition."

An arm goes round me in a friendly way, indulgently. They're so kind, North Americans. They understand anything you tell them.

I think I've got the picture now. I and the infant teachers talk long together after school at the two-foot square table laden with everything several bookshelves could take if we had them. Theirs, mine and the children's too. About the necessity of routine for stability, about freedom of the mind within the shape of order, about the organic shape of a morning supplying this routine and order, about responsibility being an ingredient of freedom and about the nature of discipline.

"Anything involving force," they argue, "of course defeats itself."

"I'm not talking about force," I say. "I'm talking about supplying the conditions for work. In particular, the disorder of the morning when we are working on the K.V. The operation of the Key Vocabulary in its pure form is clinical, classical and contemplative."

. . . About the shock to the children at beginning a new kind of school, unready for them, like going up in an airplane before it is finished, and about intoxication. "We'll start all over again tomorrow," they say.

"Step by step," another sincerely.

"We'll get everything ready."

We do get everything ready step by step and start off, but one of the teachers suddenly decides she wants to fire the clay and that all the children should see it. In a flash the infant room is empty, the morning too, so that I walk away over the snow.

In this swift age of technology, a new kind of influence on the mind of our child has emerged to replace the native imagery; the screen, radio and stereo. Nature isn't prepared for this sort of thing and is caught with her defenses down. We hear how irregular our youth is these days, but you can also read from Cicero two thousand years ago how irregular youth was in his day, and so we say, "Oh, human nature hasn't changed." But the youth in Cicero's age, in Roman times, in Elizabethan and Victorian times, and even as late as forty years ago did not encounter this replacement of the imagery. Nature was not caught by this new influence with her defenses down. It's no good saying, "Oh, human nature hasn't changed": if we're not careful, human nature *could change* —if it has not, in advance positions, already done so.

As our child sits hour after hour before the man-made screen, as the radio intrudes on the background of his mind or as the rabble-rousing beat of the latest hit booms through the trembling house, it is not that the channel outward is blocked to his imagery; it is that his defenseless mind, the frail, unique human marvel of his living feeling, is bombarded into sedation by overstimulation or even into extinction . . . none of which happened in Cicero's day.

The native imagery is being replaced by outside imagery concocted by man. It might be very good imagery too, but you can get too much of it. In all of it there is one thing wanting: it doesn't happen to be alive. It could fuse with the native imagery and become alive . . . if there were any native imagery left.

It is dead but it replaces the living pictures of the more vulnerable instincts: the compassion, pity, mercy, tenderness and the contagion of warm feeling. The screen imagery can be proved to be excellent stuff but it's not fuel that makes things go.

Our child no longer feels with love or with hatred; he does not feel at all. With the third dimension muted or erased, we get a small person with two dimensions and that's how he stays for life. He thinks and does only what he's told to or what he copies from someone else, and when we've got a lot of carbon copies of a thing we get conformity. And when we've got widespread conformity we can be told as a nation what to do and we'll obey. Can be shown how to do it and we'll copy. A nation would be led into anything.

I can't say we're in this condition yet but we could be in future years.

.   .   .

You don't get far without a dream to lure. A dream keeps you looking forward, whereas the dreamless are inclined to look backward on some former dream defused. Dreams are a living picture in the mind generating energy. They are at once direction finders and sources of power. A dream makes a life worthwhile. Life takes its quality from the glow of a dream. You can lie awake at night beneath the weight of a thousand atmospheres if there is no dream to lure; to look ahead to, plan for, fill your mind with, pretend to be real. To dream what you will do tomorrow, next week, next year and of what you hope the future brings, something that sings. You cannot sleep without the arms of a dream enclosing you between the sheets; you get out of bed and make the tea wondering whence the universe, why there is life without the comfort of a dream.

But where do you find the capacity to dream: is it something in a shop to be bought; is it a jewel to be stolen, a prize in a lottery to be won? Are dreams a commodity to be borrowed from a neighbor when your iron fuses, fabrics to be bargained for at a stall in the street, pieces to be assembled like the toy part of a rocket; are they a recipe to be studied and cooked in an oven or do they abide at the end of a rainbow?

Dreams are a blast from the living imagery exploding with profligacy. There are no limits to the dreams a mind can conceive, but only the whole mind has the mechanism to dream. We need to dream. It's somewhere to go . . . into a dream . . . if you're prepared for return to reality. Like sitting on a seat at an airport to rest. Man does not live by bread alone but by dreams also. Yet no dreams combust from imagery which is sedated or dead; not the kind with the power to lure you. Man does not die from breadlessness but from dreamlessness also. Only the smell of decomposition haunts the house where once dreams were born. Boredom is the occupier now who swallows up life in a yawn.

And above it all, the gentle eternal stars.

—JULES LAFORGUE

Peter usually speaks with vehemence or not at all, more often not at all. He's a shy boy, but when affronted he's not. There's such an uproar in the art room I must go in . . . something less than hilarious. I'm still too new to divine at once the exact source of it, not yet knowing the children well. There's action assuredly but not quite art. "The shouters will need to go," I advise, "so the others can paint," and I do edge a few of them out. The ones with the wilder voices, and Peter's is the wildest. Just through the door, that's all, until they cool off. I forget the part about force.

Touch the true voice of feeling and it will create its own style and vocabulary. The words which caption the native imagery I call the Key Vocabulary, for they unlock the mind. Any variation of the pattern of the flow from the inside outward indicates to me some variation in his life from the norm: sometimes an inner tension contracting the channel outward, maybe something alarming him; some current turbulence in his feeling . . . maybe some memory.

Wondering what is disturbing Peter, I take my folder and look up his K.V.: "Jonathon," "Peter," "car," "Michael," "Jonathon," "junk." Except for his own name, Peter, nothing from home.

After recess during the Intake hour, I remember and look round for him, for his passionate brown eyes, perfect teeth and his admirable fingers: one of the very few who are dark. Yes, there he is sitting in the arms of one of the women teachers, his favorite spot if he can make it; he even leaned against me one day. But he doesn't snuggle up to the men or tie himself round Carl's neck.

He is reading but not with absorption. His eyes glance up often to those around him, flashingly on guard, then lower again to his book. Half his mind alerted. Someday when I know him better and he knows me better . . . but any question can be an intrusion. I prefer to wait till people tell me things because they are moved to.

K.V. first thing in the morning. Where is everyone? Some are here, not all. Open the door, peer round on the plain. Yes, there are several children on the big rock punctuating the snow. Gelo and followers. The ones who are most often absent. How wonderful to be a boy on the plain, playing on a rock in the winter sun surrounded by gleaming snow. These are all right with Carl, so I too put on my coat and boots to be a boy in the snow, another of Gelo's followers. Play helicopters with them and pick up their words on a card from my pocket. Not unexpectedly, Gelo's is "helicopter" from his sentence, "The helicopter got shot down." I write "helicopter" on the rock as well; the one word will do.

Most mornings, I manage to pull this off, following the boys. They move to a drain on the plain digging industriously—or, rather, Gelo digs industriously with the one spade, inspired by a dream in his mind of something I can't see, while the others watch and comment at length. One morning they cart out the hammers, find stray timber, our own timber ends, and build steadily while their words travel from "helicopters" and "gunships" to "play school house," which changes to a fort in a matter of minutes, then to a prison and ends up as "bridge." "You be the radio reporter," they say.

Most mornings. But not a morning goes by when I do not record on my folder the newest words of the K.V., sitting at the two-foot by the window searching for some pattern in them to enlighten me. But for a few exceptions, the first words of our younger children are anything but from the inside out. Instead, a baffling array of outside words with little reference to their origins, and not so easily spoken, not so willingly, so that Carl becomes restless and doubtful, suspecting force somewhere. Yet he looks just as keenly as I do for genuine key words and none is more attuned to our children than he.

Neither are they always remembered the next day, routine casualties, and often so reluctantly written they are often not written at all. But I do take into account their resistance to handwriting anyway . . . it's conceivable that handwriting is doomed . . . which surprises me, for they draw well enough, when they do. Writing is drawing, after all.

All are on the K.V. now, the younger twenty or so; some with Carl and some with me. A matter of their personal choice. Carl sometimes writes two words instead of one, which is an acceptable variation, part of that adaptation of the use of the formula to suit different children. Like not taking their fingers to trace the letters. These do not appear to need this as other children have. I'd rather do so, however; you can read a child like an easy book by leading a small finger. Some are leadable, some are not, and all told in a finger.

Children with Carl:

ISADORE: *walked, my sister, witch, out of gas, my Dad.*

JACKY: *puppies, wrestle, house, motel, spook, tummy, tickle, new house, eat Carl, King's castle, pocket knife, Panda Bear, eyes.* (Jacky began school at seven, with a lead of two years over the fives.)

DURLA: *Gelo, baby, Manly, Gemmy, Beta, bull, squeak, new tooth, guinea pig's baby, Indian costume, my blankey.*

JAY: *Grandma Ann, hopper, witch, goblin, pink chalk, sister, woof man, pancakes, shark, Riverside, Valencia, mouses, creeper.*

GEMMY: *May* (mother), *Lily* (sister), *Mexo, Dular, deer, hampster, Letty, teddy bear, horse, bluebird, tunnel.*

MUSKIE: *corral, horse, Jove's eight puppies, Jove, pig, my sock, loft.*

JONATHON: *stuck, helicopter, blood, wood, chalk-peeler, ski-boots, tiger, no chalk, no, Monty-my-love, Mommy, red tractor, my bread bird, my lion, my Daddy, my love Jacky.*

MONTY: *house, Daddy, the East, house, pick-up truck, farm, Pancake, candy, castle, moo, Gelo's bike.*

GERALD: *Daddy, helicopter, dump truck, rabbit foot, telescope, rocket, Jotty, truck, Sola, straw, stop, Mommy, Fraser, bird, fight.*

JENNIFER: *flower, Milly, Daddy, Mommy, flower, Dick Haydon, colored chalk, dolly, devil.*

AGAR: *eyes open, I wish we had an empty room.*

MITCHELL: *Monty, no-no words, tickle, guppie, trolley.*

And with me, fewer children:

ROCKY: *Janice* (mother), *fun house, car, Frank, Russell, funny.*

GELO: *bike, Peter, Mrs. Henderson, helicopter, play school house, cat fish, jet, Christmas, snack, zoo.*

BONNIE: *Jay, Daddy, Odile, Mommy, ring, bow, house, chalkboard.*

PETER: *Jonathon, Peter, car, Michael, Jonathon, junk*

CANDY: *Beverly, Rivers Bell, Micky Moon, Chaser, Micky Moon, William* (the last four cats and dogs), *gray kitten.*

MILLY: *baby, doll, cat, Milly, puppies, balloon.*

ODILE: *Waring, Bob, Harry, Janet* (all family names), *King* (dog), *Janet, Bunza* (cat).

ANNABELLE: *Rachel, tooth, barnyard, marmalade, puppies, doll, Lizza had puppies, marmalade, bunny, wolf, loose toenail.*

I examine these words of a new generation of North Americans recorded hastily on a large folder each day, looking and looking for an overall pattern I can hang an answer on. A

handle to get hold of. What is easily available is the minimum of words from home in the total and little sign of the
inside-outside flow of the K.V. as you get with most children;
or indeed of any overall current. The words seem to wave
about independent of emotion's origin.

Some trends do show, however: the passing of Halloween has left its trail of words—"witch," "spook," "Indian
costume," "goblin," "pig," "my lion," "candy," "rabbit foot,"
"devil," "bunny," echoing the exuberant Halloween party
which took over the school.

Also the talk of dogs: without any counting up, one sees
the foremost interest . . . dogs and their puppies. It is love,
anyway, and for something at home. These dogs are obviously genuine key words and I've never seen this score before. Dogs in this town are just like people, are treated like
people and act like people, even to attending their own school,
and all but talk the language. All big dogs they are, who
bark at my coat but so far have not bitten me. For my own
interest, I compare the surfacing of five words:

Own name	2
helicopter	3
Daddy	7
Mommy	8
dogs	15

which no doubt would impress the dogs.

A variation on the key vocabulary. I recall taking word
scores from small Maori children, at the tail end of civilization, when it was the fright and sex words which won . . .
though there were dogs enough about. "Ghost" and "kiss"

came up most strongly. Where are the fear and sex words here? Perhaps they will turn up later. Yet I don't know. A feature of these young children is their lack of malice. There's plenty of sex among them, though it does not come up in the K.V. Why not?

A fascinating variation, but I'm still a new girl serving my apprenticeship in a new culture, having little to say other than that statistics don't reveal the man. Word scores so far don't show motives, which would appear to be "Have a good time." It's just this little matter of the best way to have a good time which so often leads to boredom. All roads lead to boredom except work, the bedrock of life's logic.

I do ponder, however, on the story the K.V. tells me of this particular society, the post-industrial, advance-guard point of it; why it varies so from the norm of a happy child. It could be any one or all of a number of reasons: the inside words have been covered before they came to school; intoxication from the heady drink of freedom for which they were not prepared; the native imagery has been bombarded by overstimulation into silence and stillness, or has already been replaced by the lifeless man-made concoction, so that some of the children are a dimension short; the agitation of our children at a new school and new teachers or the agitation of the race itself.

To me, an alien, there is no telling as I footprint the snow. One night over supper, I pose the question to a local writer, "Which is it, then?"

"It's the agitation of the race itself."

Another night the same question to a local doctor, who unhesitatingly replies, "It's the agitation of the race itself," again. North Americans themselves should know. From which arises the chilling possibility that in the Key Vocabulary our children of the new generation are writing on the wall the future of my host nation.

Weeks more of unconnected words like limbs detached from a body waving independently, hilariously, while further ways puzzle me: they never ask questions . . . why not? No one goes through my handbag which I leave accessible. Did anyone hear of a five-year-old not going through a handbag when he had the chance? Why don't they dash outside to play, to break clear of architectural confinement, or do they like confinement? They play inside all right most brightly, play house, play shop vividly; wrestle, roll, run and creep, or act out terrifyingly real boys' imagery behind closed doors and form dark clubs in the library. But show them a door outside? "I've got a cold."

"My mother said I'm sick."

"I can't find my gloves."

Such wonderful soft snow in the sun and they've got warm clothes, the latest in parkas and boots, and they're all for going skiing in the afternoon or ice-skating at the rink. They don't have colds then, are not said to be sick, and can usually find their gloves as well as their ski poles. Yet here they all are packed into this hot, close, overbreathed air with walls every way you turn, nylon-lit. What about the fresh white air outside and the jet-shot blue sky? "You little people can run outside."

"I dowanna."

Some of them love to settle down at a low table with paper and crayons to draw and draw and draw. Together. Glancing across cozily at each other's work. Comfortably

and happily. My God, the acres of paper to a non-American
The forests of it. I tell Carl, "I find this paper waste very
hard to take."

"Plenty more where that came from."

Why, but for a few, do they reject responsibility to one
another, obligation to one another: "Who will share his
snack with Rocky? He hasn't got any."

Silence from the banquet, then a single voice sepul-
chrally, "Nobody."

Unbelieving, I ask it again. "Who will share his snack
with Rocky?"

A collective chorus, "Nobody!"

Not all reject responsibility. No blanket statement for
these freedom children. Isadore, the warm one, has the job of
caring for the smallest and newest; the Grade 2 girls are responsible people and pleasant to turn to. But I have not yet
succeeded in any degree in coaxing the fives to work with one
another, hear one another their words in twos and threes and
teach one another. "These are *my* words. You can't have
them." Not all, but most. Cooperation seems deeply missing.
Not without note, it is often those with key home words who
can work with each other. Durla will hear another his words,
Bonnie consents to be heard while Jacky doesn't find that it
kills him. But so far for most it's the wannadowanna, the new
contagious religion: me first and only, you not at all. Solo is
the word. Solo living.

And to their equipment. Hell, the protest when it's time
to do their appointed jobs, and pick up their paper. But who
could keep up with the frothing paper streaming from room
to room? It's bedazzling. And there's plenty more for tomorrow.

Why don't they like handwriting; is it going out? Why do some blush at the word "love"; is love going out? Why are they reluctant to build with the timber; would they rather have shiny blocks? Having been read a story, why don't they comment spontaneously and ask questions like mad at the finish; ask questions at all? Why do many skip from one medium to another during the Output period; from paint to clay, from clay to sand, from sand to the water tank, without finishing things? Not all, but many.

Criticism from a new girl doesn't weigh much. . . . I have more in appreciation. The way they can listen to a story however long, however hard, however boring at times, in unmoving sustained attention. Without exception they like to pick up a book and turn over the pages; the actual speaking of everyone shows that speaking is not going out, while their debating powers show that brains are not out; all are simply lovely to look at, none intentionally breaks a thing; although they quarrel with ability, one doesn't strike another although they occasionally say so; as for the overall level of intelligence, it's not going out but coming in . . . two or three years up, relatively.

But a few things I keep to myself however much wine at supper, for I do not myself yet accept them: that our children may be victimized by overstimulation, the attention span concertinaed, the third dimension erased and the vision fragmented. I keep these to myself, though I do talk over with some American friends the exact meaning of the word "mutation."

Just in case some of these secret conclusions happen to be right, I settle for some mild treatment, unostentatious and simple: I withdraw from them at school any external stimulation from record playing, let them hear only the sounds they make themselves . . . their own voices, their own singing, their own crying and playing; hide any expensive shiny toys they might bring to school, try to provide conditions in which they can make their own playthings . . . puppets, for instance, with a parent; expose them to primary elements like sand, water, mud, clay, snow and timber ends; make sure there's plenty of paints and brushes; teach those who like it primitive rhythms . . . Maori song and dance, clapping, swaying, hula and haka; compose and illustrate for them a series of graded reading books drawn from their own vocabularies . . . the themes from their own drama; let them know how much we like the plays they make; try to teach them to ask questions; teach responsibility as a separate subject in its own right and, above all, proceed with the organic program. Find the native imagery, awake it if alive and exercise it much of the time.

These twenty-two or so on the K.V. in which they supply their own words as working material, to be used later in the morning for handwriting, spelling, reading and phonics and for talking points . . . these children tell me much about themselves and display their variety. None is the same, none like another. The K.V. reveals some normal children, several disturbed and a few out-and-out originals. Also it seems to uncover new racial characteristics, reordered proportions of the personality foretelling the human future, but until the second movement at least I'll keep it to myself.

For their K.V.s do not follow the usual pattern . . . but for one or two. There is little flow, put it this way, from the inner man out; a minimum of movement in any direction, no discernible shape to the comprehensive scene. The large percentage of their words have little instinctive meaning: fears, loves, desires, hates or reeling disappointment. They cannot be two-dimensional only, but it does look something like it. I'll wait and see.

We continue on the K.V. regardless, and no less gaily than the children, hoping that captions of vital imagery will appear in more convincing proportions, more of the deep words from home, as well as words like Jonathon's "blood," Monty's "the East," where his father is, and Peter's enumeration of boys he admires but does not join . . . Jonathon and someone called Michael, outside the school. Annabelle's "loose toenail," Agar's "I wish we had an empty room" . . . we carry on while I try to divine the reasons. What is the undermind cause? I don't think the bulk of the words . . . but for a few . . . are genuine key words unlocking the mind. Don't tell me there's nothing to unlock. Except for twenty-seven captions from close on two hundred over the last few weeks, you could say we were still waiting.

By October, I register a movement in my dream of an operating infant room. The dream expands a little. Some of the young ones on the K.V. find themselves inadvertently in the second movement, the two-word captions: Rocky, Odile, Gelo, Bonnie, Peter, Milly, Candy and Henry. It is not a case of, "Oh, these have more brains than the others, therefore they are promoted." I wouldn't even say, "Oh, they have more access to themselves and their words flow freer." No, I think it's just because they've reached a certain number of words for one reason and another: being here on the spot at the time, for one; interested in what they're doing, for another. Interest and presence succeed as classmates. But it's got nothing to do with brains or access.

Actually they shouldn't be moving from one teacher to another at all . . . not that they are; I've been with them all the time from the start; in the family fluidity of my dream, as well as from custom, there's no compulsory changing of teachers. With children from four to seven, or three to seven, each teacher knows the technique of each of the movements, so that any child can go to any teacher in any of the movements. Like a family. But a spaceship isn't built for family fluidity; besides, our teachers do not yet know the techniques of all the movements. "All the movements" sounds complicated but they're all the same; they're all one flowing movement, in fact: releasing the native imagery again to use for working material, except that with an increasing facility our children use now two words, or three words or four or five, until they can write a page.

The skill itself lies in the understanding, rapport and delicacy of a teacher in talking to our children, not in how many words they use, or in what movement the child is working in. The movements are sheer convenience, interchangeable daily.

I sit on a cut-down chair in the corridor between five doors: the doorless door at the end to what they call the meeting room, where Carl works with the little ones . . . don't let me slip and say "babies" though I like the word; the art-room door to the left with the paint, sand and water; the door to the Grade 2 headquarters at my right, with the doors to the clay and the math rooms behind me. "To link us all up," I say, "to act as though we're all in one room as a family." Which seems to be acceptable. It does link us too, though it does not hide from me that I have a separate class; the worst disgrace an infant teacher can have . . . a class. Moreover, along with the three doors, we're on the freeway to both bathrooms and the storeroom as well, so there's much coming, going, passing and stepping over. We see quite a bit of the senior school—of their legs and feet, that is—and quite a bit of the legs and feet of teachers, parents and office workers, not to mention the visitors.

You could be excused for thinking that this is martyr's talk and that I don't like it, but as it happens I do; who am I to quarrel with being in the center of the vortex of interweaving life, blasting, inter-rocketing life? I've always liked international air terminals. As for our children, they simply don't notice it. This condition would be the ideal excuse for our children not working together and I should use it, except that it's not the reason. Theoretically, according to the image in my own mind, the children with me are hearing one another while waiting for their turn to come to me, but it doesn't come off. And it's not because of the through traffic. "Come on, Rocky, Gelo. Sit like this facing each other, so that your knees touch, and hear each other your words."

"I would like to go outside now and play on the big rock and make a helicopter and . . ." from Gelo.

"Big rock," I say.

"Gelo can't hold my words," from Rocky, and retreats to the arms and knees of a teacher on the floor, where he is heard his words solo and in comfort. "Who wants my words?" from Gelo, scattering them in a shower over the others. "I'm gonna play on the rock."

In mind I see an infant room of the past, a large, tall,

spacious room, a vivid moving family of fifty, groups of small children reading to each other their own work and reading each other's work zestfully; all manner of verbal and hand illustration in stand-up action, with no teacher among them until I am free. No force or anything like that: just routine, stability and a shape to the morning. But our infant-room teachers do not and cannot hold the dream I do. It's possible that all this looks good to them . . . no *force* and all that, all freedom. The reason for the difference, however, between then and now comes through to me as I sit thinking in the heart of the vortex, the still center: there, where a human dream was fertilized and which materialized, was the tail end of civilization, whereas here, a corridor in a physics building, is the nosepoint of civilization where few if any dreams exist to be fertilized, much less to materialize.

I've lately said that I've always liked international air terminals, but this crossroads of five doors, two bathrooms and a storeroom, of eight directions, is, intellectually and spiritually, not an international air terminal but an interplanetary space terminal where this new generation of humans is deciding which route it will take: back to nature and caves or ahead into space. Neither do nor can the young staff share this vision with me. And if I ever had any criticism of young North American graduates it would be this: the atrophy of dream and vision.

I sit in my cut-down chair thinking, dreaming and seeing while the traffic edges by; not only the regular traffic but the really lovely movement of our children themselves, past me to the clay room maybe, to the math room where the rods and puzzles are, or just past me anyway . . . to wonderfully explore the other end of the ship where the older children are, and the office where parents are and the telephone with access to home . . . the eddying of people and children round me like turbulent restless waters. Vividly I am seeing that residue of the human race which remains on the Earth obeying Life's laws in order to live fully; then I see the advance guard of evolution which has taken off per spaceship to a distant planet of the galaxy which I have named Cosmet, there to reject the laws of Life and to wallow in the wannadowanna.

"Who is coming to me first?" I ask, although I'd rather call clearly, "Peter, come to me." We like to call and be called; it means we want and are wanted. Fancy my trying to justify to myself why I'd rather say, "Peter, come to me," than the Who will . . . ? sort of thing. Who will . . . ? slams a decision before our child to be made before he considers work. Just say, "Here's our work; do it." Or "Peter, come to me." The direction is clear and the intention is uncluttered, but none of this mixes with Authority and Equality and the suspicion in the word "Force."

As it happens, several do cluster up round me, but it's no good saying, "What do you want to say today," not to these who do not have easy access to themselves, when they have selves to have access to. Here is called for an adaptation of the application of the axiomatic formula: "Release the native imagery of our child and use it for working material." These children take some time, comparatively, to know what they want to say. You engage them in conversation until they do. "Your dress is the same color as my blouse," to Odile.

"Always I like this color."

"I like other colors better but this orange looks nice with my brown smock."

"My Mommy buyed this in Cornerwood, and she kept

it for a surprise for me. She hanged it in the wardrobe and I didn't know!"

"The other dresses must have got a surprise too. What did they say?"

"I don't know."

"I do."

She laughs in her quick way. "No, you don't. You weren't there, Mrs. H."

"I didn't have to be. Somebody else told me what they said. Your yellow parka there on the peg. I heard her saying to Candy's parka, 'Guess what,' and Candy's parka said, 'What?' and your parka said, 'Odile's mother bought her a new dress in Cornerwood and hid it in the wardrobe. It's orange.' And her green dress said, 'Who are you?' "

" 'I came from Cornerwood,' said the orange."

" 'You think you're smart because you came from Cornerwood?' "

" 'You've got to come from somewhere,' replied the orange."

" 'Poof,' said the green. 'I came from a shop at Jacksonville. That's further than Cornerwood.' "

" 'That's nothing,' said the red dress. 'I came from Clutha.' "

"No," joins in Odile, "my red dress didn come from Clutha. My Nanny sent me that from New York. And my green dress didn't come from Jacksonville; it was made here."

"See?" I agree. "You can't always believe what dresses say. But your purple dress said, 'Odile likes me best.' "

" 'How do you know?' says Orange."

" 'Because she wore me on Thanksgiving Day.' "

" 'She wore me,' says Green, 'on Halloween Eve.' "

" 'But she wore *me*,' says Red, 'to school for a week.' "

"And now," from Odile, glowing, "I'm going to wear Orange for two weeks."

"Hurray! I'll wear my orange blouse for two weeks in that case. To be a mate for your dress."

Odile spreads the short skirt of her orange dress. "My dress," with feeling.

"My dress," I print on the long card, yellow for the convenience of grouping, and off she goes happily to write it. Gelo has not taken off to play on the big rock yet, Milly is eying warily the two parkas hanging on adjacent pegs and Bonnie has her ear to them. "They're still talking," she reports.

"I'm next," says Gelo, scenting entertainment, but Peter says vehemently, "I'm next," and Henry says, "No, me."

Though largely the imagery remains peripheral, I do get the feeling of something stirring in our children, as though occupants in the mind house were waking. Not exactly a movement from the inside out, but a movement of some kind on the fringe. Could it be from the outside inward; what next? In what was only a little over a week, the two-word captions on the yellow cards show:

PETER: *black crayon, Green River, good picture, hairy gorilla, Halloween, wicked witch.*
Good picture and black crayon. He's always drawing in the Grade 2 room instead of going outside. Hairy gorilla? Could be a symbol of what is frightening him keeping half his mind alerted and his talking vehement.

Halloween, wicked witch . . . he's anticipating Halloween, which must be profoundly moving him.

"Rocky?" one snowing morning, "come to me."

"No, no," shrilly, "not today. I'm playing with Henry."

"You'll have nothing new to read after recess."

"I dowanna write today. It's vacation day." Carried away poetically with the novel idea, "Vacation Day!" at the top of his voice. "Vacation, Vacation Day!"

"We'll write 'Vacation Day.'"

"I'm going to have Vacation Day. Wow! Vacation Day," which I write on his card.

ROCKY: *I'm happy, play dough, Vacation Day, pocket knife, lumber jacket, wild buffalo.*

BONNIE: *cherry pie, my finger, my Mommy, Senta (mother), my nose, my chair, the sun.*

HENRY: *our puppies, bad Arab, bumble bee, yellow fellow, ice skating.*

ODILE: *my dress, my lamp, my ring, my coat, my hook, my book, my dolls.*

All as it should be in a contented child. Having surfaced all the loves of her family, then her dogs and cats, now her own possessions important to her. The way the "my" comes up . . .

MILLY: *my puppies, my feet, my dog, baby guppies.*

Her concern for small things: baby earlier in the K.V., now the puppies and baby guppies. She's a small slight girl herself.

CANDY: *gold fish, pretty fairy, pin cat, princess, snow flake, that zebra.*

Candy often dresses up at school, putting on the tulle dress to be a fairy and the lace dress to be a princess. The "pin cat" is a brooch she wore to school in the form of a cat. She probably dresses and undresses more than anyone I know except a granddaughter of mine called Kirstine. They both love clothes, as Odile does, but it comes up in their words in different ways, which is a thing one is constantly reminded of when working organically with children: the uniqueness of each child: the frail, unique human marvel of each young mind.

GELO: *new parka, rattle snake, new boots.*

The new parka and new boots are symbols, I think, of the excitement of afternoon skiing when parents take them off. The rattlesnake he was telling me about he claims he saw on the plain. A circumstance I take personal note of, having come from a snakeless country. I cross-questioned him about it at the time.

The proportion is a little better. Peter, Candy, Henry and Gelo still gambol on the periphery, but others are moving nearer home. Up comes Rocky's instinct for poetry in "I'm happy." Bonnie is still relaxed in symbiosis with her mother: three times now her mother comes up; first in the K.V. and now two days running in "my Mommy" and "Senta," her mother's name. Her mother is on the staff and she has access to her all day. Some people argue for symbiosis, our child being with her mother all day; some say it is best to have a break in order to appreciate the mother in reunion; in London, some young people prove that a child's worst enemy is his or her mother, claiming that mothers absorb the souls of their children on the grounds of womb ownership, and that children should be removed at birth and given away, while in

Israel many of the young do remove their children at birth and give them away to be brought up by others. Each to his own, I'd say. But whatever the rearing of our child there is always the safety valve of organic work to draw off any toxin.

And Milly with her "my feet," "my puppies," "my dog." My. And Odile runs true to course. All these observations, along with the accumulation of the rich word "my," stir up my dream of an infant room full and whole, with the outbreak of dancing recurringly, singing . . . music from ourselves . . . in which events happen and grow and expand and bloom, where the creative channel expands wide open and the destructive one closes. Not that I see any serious destructive channel to be closed in our children; the worst I see is a quarrelsomeness and an uneasy discontent, but I've got more thinking to do on this. One thing I'm sure of is that my dream is changing, that it will end up something else; some infant room, not from the tail end of civilization, but extraordinarily of the nosepoint. A shape beyond the present.

None mentions the snow which began two months ago, not like the impact of Halloween. Only Henry mentioned ice-skating and Candy snowflake, though most are skiing or skating every afternoon, while the corridor is a place for skis and skates and radiant with skiing clothes. Even I wrote verses about the snow and what it does to me.

Yes, there's a faint stirring. Though some show no particular direction either way, anyway, I do sense new movement; not from the inside out but from the outside inward, which I've got to believe whether I can read it or not. Not that I count or enumerate the words . . . just get the feeling.

It is also true that our children are printing better, managing the two-word sequences with the space between and knowing what they mean. It's important about the quality of the printing, this being the medium of communication when they read their work to each other, and it is likely to be good, considering the drawing they do instead of playing outside, especially Peter's. I wish Peter were one of these who come to me, but no; it's the arms and knees of an American teacher on the corridor floor with us. He might tell me one day what frightens him, so that I could understand his fragmented concentration on anything he does. But that will be when *he* comes to *me*; not I to him.

Most of our children are plainly settling better, getting the hang of the routine and knowing what's next. A minimum of confrontations, less inverted authority. During the Output period, the first hour and a half, you should see the painting at the ten-child easel, the playing and pouring in the water tank, exchanging soft secrets, the concentrated engineering in the sand tank . . . tunneling, constructing and composing scapes; the hands a-passion in the clay room modeling tirelessly; only music is missing, and the dancing. It's refreshing to cruise through this end of the ship seeing all of each child in action; his head, his heart, his hands and his tongue. And all of each teacher. Among.

This interplanetary intersection I'm paid to patrol. If you lowered your sights to the pinpoint present, you might risk the sin of boredom, whereas in exercising the antennae . . . wondering on mutations in men, galaxial gradations or culminations on Cosmet . . . you risk only misunderstanding, of which you run into volumes down here on the maligned good old Earth, in the changes, exchanges and interchanges between rampaging ogres by the misnames of Authority and Equality; not to overlook their offspring, wee wannadowanna . . . all of which is expensive on Valium. Actually, there's just as good and much cheaper a sedative gratuitously granted by Mars: lift your sights above it all to the gentle eternal stars.

I Don't
Want
to work

It is Isadore who writes, "I Don't Want to work," but at least she gets this written. A glamorous mercurial character whose medium is her tongue. Why write when you know you can capture your audience with vivid talk? Actually I think her medium is dance, but there's no room and no piano in the stern. She's naturally dramatic and, if she finds life not exactly as she wants it, is eloquent with picturesque excuses and elongated absences. And none of us persuades but greets her warmly when she reappears. She's one of these originals who give me a lead, although we have not yet achieved in the chock-a-block cabins the desired family fluidity Isadore has, floating from one teacher to another at will in the most classical way, with a book in each movement, so that in the action and bustle of the mornings you don't know whether she's had her words or not. You know only that she has less than anyone else. And who wants to capture and harness a wildly free spirit? And how often have I used the word "beautiful" when describing these children?

When she writes "I Don't Want to work," she really means, I think, "I don't want to write." Few do, so that I conjecture that writing is going out. Talk, telephone, dictaphone and tape recorder take the place of writing. At this planetary intersection, our children are choosing their own directions whatever I do about it. Writing is not for Isadore and she makes this plain. Her hands are so small, for instance.

I still think, however, that our writing could be better if for reading purposes only, as a medium of communication, in order that one can read his writing to another; so that there's a point in writing after all, telling another something on paper, and I begin taking rather formal handwriting lessons after recess during the Intake period: I sitting in the dim-lit corridor on the cut-down chair and they grouped on the floor before me with lined paper and pencils, using small blackboards on their knees for tables . . . all as the traffic flows by. Steps by, over, round and through us gently enough. No one gets trodden on, pushed or bumped. To see each other, you merely look round someone's leg or wait till it's passed.

I enjoy these lessons a lot anyway, putting limbs on the letters, filling in their faces, standing them on their heads and supplying dialogue like an impromptu entertainment screen, with the difference that our children take part too. "Mrs. H.," from O, "I hate being on this paper."

"Why, little O?"

"Because of those kids down there."

"There's nothing wrong with these kids, they're friends of mine."

"Okay, but they're not friends of mine."

"What have you got against them, O?"

"It's that boy with the blue sweater. He stares at me."

"See-see," from Gelo, "I stare because you've got arms and legs."

"Why shouldn't I have arms and legs, Gelo? You have."

"But letters don't have arms and legs and faces, and that's why I stare."

"I have *every right* to have arms and legs," indignantly from O. "How can I ride your bike if I haven't got legs?"

"Oh, little O," I reprove, "so you've been riding Gelo's bike."

"Of course I've been riding his silly bike. It's easy. Both the wheels are like me . . . they're round. Look, look, Mrs. H. That's why I hate those kids. They're laughing at me."

Hastily redrawing O's mouth, "But you're laughing at them."

Oh, yes, I enjoy these lessons just to hear the children laugh. I know I'm only a TV screen, but I'm having fun myself. It is how teaching will be done on Cosmet. Amusement value, no personal effort, no doing work for the sake of the work itself. No sacrifice, no sweat. Inadvertent learning.

At the end of these lessons, one of the children takes the teacher's chair to judge whose writing is good enough to take home and whose is not. One in judgment over another, which it is claimed they hate. But it goes all right. We don't mind.

Sometimes one of the children sits in the chair and takes the lesson himself, and I'm on the floor with the others, so that my writing also goes up for inspection to take home or not take home. But mine is so bad . . . my letters skipping all over the page, rolling and somersaulting. . . .

"Mrs. H.," from the teacher, "you can't take yours home."

"Why not?" affronted.

"Because all your letters are crazy, crazy."

I whine, "Can't I take my writing home. . . ."

"No, it's not good enough, right?"

I act convincing crying.

"Okay, okay, if you're going to cry, take it then." Passes it back.

My face lights up in a sunny smile as I reach for it.

Snatches it back. "No, you can't!"

Upon which I fall to crying again dolefully, while most of the others laugh like anything. Where is their compassion?

"Yes, you can. Here, take it home."

I reach out, suddenly smiling.

"No, you can't!" snatching it back, and again the sad crying. I warm up making it real to the children's merry laughter. Gleeful it is. Cackling like Cosmet people at the distress of another; mercy and pity withered away centuries ago. These have chosen their direction.

Suddenly there's a swoop from the Grade 2 room and here is Angela. Sits on my knees, embracing me, comforting and stroking. "You're hurting her," weeping, "you're hurting her!" Mercy has survived in Angela. It will be the Angelas and their seed remaining on the Earth. I have just build, "Cackling like Cosmet people at the distress of another"; rather, "Cackling like Cosmet people at the *exposure* of another's feeling." The script demands it.

I sense that we're all playing roles. Mercy has survived. The Goodies won. The teacher lets me have my work to take home. The TV show is over and we drop to reality, bump clumsily down to reality, which happens to be reading of the native imagery released in words and written this morning to be used for working material. Carl lets his little ones go, and we come into the meeting room away from the traffic. We read also from the set of graded readers I'm making for them, the vocabulary drawn from their own and the themes from their own drama. After which Carl reads everyone a story. Everyone who happens to be still here, I mean.

To go back a few weeks, to catch up on all that's happened, and on my thoughts:

The end of October. Four weeks of it. We have run through the organic program in an outline sort of way, but only I hold the real thing in mind. We have run through it before until it fell beneath the clay-firing day but we have been steadily rebuilding. The young teachers are longing to get it right, mold a steady shape, and the routine is steadily stabilizing. Output for the first half of the morning, releasing the native imagery in any media we can lay our hands on; the *use* of it for the second half of the morning is the leading idea.

But our children do not at all find it easy learning new routine, along with everything else that's new; but it will grow progressively easier as the routine clarifies and deepens, as the tendons of the morning strengthen like cross reference in a manuscript. Not yet have we got to the stage where you can leave any one group to work on its own so that you can attend to another. They have to be looked after all the time like little babies of three, unable to interest themselves on their own, to work creatively together. There is available quite a selection of media, but they cannot settle to it, and when we come in after recess for the Intake . . . those who do come in . . . instead of going for it, settling down eagerly to read their own words and hear each other in a friendly way, they look for reasons not to. They are still quarrelsome and discontented unless they have a teacher's whole attention exclusively for themselves. You'd think many of them had never had any babying and mothering at all and were making up for lost love, yet from my regular interviewing of parents and dining with the families I know this is not the case. Not only no responsibility to others but a minimum to themselves. I can't make out why. But obviously the days are steadier than they were and we can only keep on trying.

The last day of October. Ideas for today: three words on paper for the second movement spearing into the third. It's time we went into books. I can't find anything like the books I want in the local shops, so I'll have to make them myself. Now how can I make these books by Monday? But, remembering the click of the heels to attention and the Heil Hitler salute, I decide to make them myself.

Little blue books for the new third movement. I make them at school before school. Six small writing books with lined paper, with covers of thick blue. And blue cards in place of

123

the yellow. During the Output period, I introduce these books to six small children: Odile five, Rocky five, Gelo six, Peter five, Milly five, Bonnie four. To me it's my first solid footing on the organic work. Specific. I make a blue box to keep the books and cards in, in the interests of order and identity.

Henry is so often not here, tracking Zed Zane, that he can stay in the second movement; so can Candy, who, in the new freedoms, is disengaging from groups and works on her own more, often alone in the clay room. She's a girl who is never idle and teaches herself, and none of us overlooks the value of this.

Sitting together in the corridor highway linking the five other rooms, we move from the two-word captions . . ."my dress," "play dough," "wild buffalo" and such . . . to three words or more, which I write on their blue cards, showing the further spacing. As it is at last the greatly anticipated Halloween, the subject runs: "I'm an Indian," "I'm a duck," "I'm a Mexican," "Trick or treat," "I'm going to be a clown." Witches, devils and spooks, I notice, are surfacing in the second movement and the K.V. with Carl.

For this half hour or more, we have something like a lesson, our children intent on their work. At last we've struck oil . . . access to powerful and living imagery. No need to engage in elaborate conversation until they speak with feeling. As it has been in the past with other children, only "And what's for you?"

"Trick or treat."

Like old times in another society. It's taken four weeks to arrive at this, an orderly lesson. Orderly because of the power of the native imagery in collective energy. We could do with small tables and chairs for this writing with pencils in their books, but small blackboards on their knees suffice. Improvisation hurts no one. Making do. The Halloween party planned for the afternoon is blowing up and starting under its own power early in the morning, whirling dressing-up action all round us, noise ceiling high, grownups and children stepping over and round us with practiced agility, but the writers intent on what they're writing, in the thick of it. Five heads down to it . . . Bonnie has deserted . . . intent on the discharge of the imagery into words.

Then the whole school blows up in a party.

I've left the ship. Into the cold sun and over the snow to the skeleton of the music tent. Among the bare cottonwoods. The mountains are bare too but for snow on the higher slopes. The air amazingly mellow for the end of October. Glancing back at the humble row of rooms of the physics building, I wonder if they've pulled themselves together, if they mean to. If they've pulled the morning together. It's too late to pull the shape together; it's shattered. Obviously Carl both sees and cares. The wannadowanna raging out of control . . .

Pacifying to walk out here alone, in silence. The snow, the tall mountains, the white keen air. You can think out here. You can't think in centrally heated, carbon-dioxided, carpeted encapsulation. The high, overheated, overpitched emotions flaring in personalities with tongues like pocket-knives would never endure in the wide fresh air. It's like a hothouse back there . . . dreamlike, nightmarish at times, unreal. A half-lit TV serial. Sanity takes leave and goes for a walk.

.   .   .

I come back and they're all at snack in carnival dress-up. Temporarily contained. As I enter the swinging door, Senta touches me. "What sort of a morning are you having?"

"I felt like going away and never coming back."

"So did I. I said to them, 'I'm going away and I'm not coming back.' And when I did come back they were nervously quiet."

I don't go among them but leave them to the others. The Americans know them better. I've got to collect the new words from the K.V. this morning and the two-word captions, so I sit at what I call my table and get out my folder. At least I'm by the window with a slit of cold air. I don't closely know what happens to the rest of the day. Children do come in from time to time to show me their costumes but I don't rave. Halloween words . . . A great wave of emotion sweeping over them like a *hui* in a Maori *pa*. I make them two books on Halloween.

First day of November. For the third time, we rebuild the organic shape of the morning, shattered twice. We've been born a month. I suppose we are better. We do at least see again the outline of the morning, but there's much not accomplished. The K.V. did not fit too well for a start on these new children, but with American Carl's hand on it it's better than it was. Over all, the captions in the first and second movements are less a record of what they are than a record of their agitation. I prefer to think it is a transient agitation at the big changes in their lives, but who am I to come to conclusions after one month? As I've said, a local doctor and a local writer think otherwise, that it's the agitation of the race itself. But I sense they are responding a little and that the vision of the five in the third movement is a little less fragmented, less so as they proceed. And I must say I'm becoming fond of them. . . .

The second day in November. Fairly good morning. Carl always does the K.V. well and the second movement. I do the third movement, but not too well. They're so different from other children with whom I have worked round the world. Usually it takes no time for children to find in themselves something important, but with these it is a long time and a long way inward. True they found the Halloween words, which had surfaced anyway, but, again, where are the fear and sex words or, put it this way, where is the evidence of their instincts? "What are you frightened of, Peter?"

"I'm not frightened."

"Whom do you love, Rocky?"

"Nobody."

"Whom do you love, Peter?"

Blushing, "Not love . . . *like*."

While waiting for their turn in the morning to come to me, other children will hear each other their words, teach each other and talk to each other about them, but not these. Not unless you sit down beside them and guide them. Somersaults or quarrels or they go away. I try turning them loose on the different media and then call them later, but they're busy by then and won't come. And it's not fair to interrupt. Cooperation is still quite missing, though concentration, sticking at a thing and finishing it, is advancing. And when they do come to me they take such a long long time over their writing that I'm not only believing that writing is going out but considering letting it go out. Such a long broken-up time over writing. Tomorrow I'll have a talk with them first about going to the other media while waiting but coming to me when I call them. Prepare them. They are reasonable people and can understand anything, more than any other children I know. Moreover, since we've been working together in the corridor . . . sometimes Candy joins, looking over my shoulder . . . a certain feeling seems to be growing between us, thank heaven.

I carry on with the series of graded books I'm making at home. They've got to have something easy enough to read, and spare us from Dick and Jane. I'm told there are no other easy enough American books available, though I can't believe it. There are in Mauritius and London and New Zealand. But even if there were, it remains true that books made from their own vocabulary, their own lives, own drama and their own locality have a natural and strong place in the organic work. I'm up to School 7 now, involving the theme of "Take me, Daddy," the theme you find most dominant anywhere, about Daddy going away from home to work or going away for good. It's a personal theme of themselves, never failing, which is the nature of organic work. The first books presenting Mommy, Daddy, baby and brothers and sisters I do not presume even to illustrate, since they are deeply key words, holding within the mind their own illustrations which no artist or screen can equal. In the meantime, I send home to New Zealand for a few dozen easy books, easy enough for three-year-olds as well as fives. . . . Our government keeps a team on its payroll for work like this, including established novelists.

Eleven-thirty of the Intake period is reading time, when

I collect every teacher I can lay my hand to, every parent in sight and every unsuspecting visitor to help with individual reading. Right or wrong, I like to see each child read each day to someone, though it hasn't come off yet. Presupposing as it does that every child is here at eleven-thirty, whereas this hasn't happened yet. You'll find some on the big rock, some in the senior science room, music room, one or two in the office with their parents and some . . . where? It's a pleasant scene, reading time, with our children nestling up to grownups on the floor, reading to them, but a pleasanter scene to me would be to see them nestling up to themselves trying to read independently. This baby way of nestling up to people, as though they'd never been weaned. Some call it emotional immaturity, but so far I hold my tongue.

Anyway, it interests me to keep a record of each book they've read on another well-used card folder. The reading record. Little people who appear not to think or write as well as they could turn out to be forward readers, telling me more about each child. Gelo finds writing hard labor, yet he and Peter take the lead in reading. I like to know where each child is and what he can do, and I like the knowing. I'm here to know and I see that I know where each one is.

In testing these new readers on the floor, you find that mistakes reveal themselves. Too-many-new-words-here sort of thing. This one not used enough and that. On the other hand, running side by side with their own organic writing, they are using words already being used, doubling on them, hard ones like "they," "you" and "are," which support each other. And you learn other things: School 8 is too hard, too long and with too many new words, a good example of a bad book, yet somehow the children race through it, the theme being the one about "my friend, my best friend, my very best friend," and I see them holding it to the very last page.

You take Jonathon, still on the K.V., who spends much time in the upper school educating himself in his own way . . . he turns up a very good reader. Durla, still on the K.V., yet here is her name at the front of the reading record card. People like Gerald you seldom see, because his mother is often working in the office; he too. You never know. Hidden abilities come to light. And the way children's progress when annotated takes the form of a spearhead: sharp at the point with one name . . . Peter; widening gradually with two behind, four behind that, then ten, then more to the wide coverage at the base. In reading or in anything else you annotate. SHAPE has ever been a big thing with me, taking as it does its outline from the variations of nature, of impulse and energy and interest, the three adding up to character. All indivisibly related to what's going on in the area of imagery, which is to say: imagery is the ovum.

Thinking further with growing momentum, you see that this overall shape of the collective impulse is the nearest nature can get to the perfect answer to the stress and strain of life. Poor old reading card, hastily entered, roughly written and increasingly dog-eared from handling . . . yet part of my own key to our children.

Affluence is one of our troubles. The thing about deprivation is that it makes you dream, and a dream is a germ of living and exercises the imagery. This is the main aim in organic work . . . to exercise the imagery to keep it alive. Keep it flexible and pulsing and in good form, active, to help us think and do things.

And here's little Muskie with a timber end, pushing it round the sand as a truck. In this he can see a truck: the wheels, the cab, the tray at the back, the man in his seat driving, and he supplies the sound of the engine. But when he brings a real toy truck to school, shiny, red wheels, the lot, he doesn't need to imagine a truck—it's all here—while his imagery settles back and withers. Lazy. Unwanted, if you like. I hide it. High on a shelf in the storeroom when he is not looking. Sometimes he and Jonathon will draw a truck . . . no, not Jonathon, who draws people . . . he and Gerald, rather, and the imagery awakes to work, driven from behind by desire. Or, when he can't find the one I've hidden, he sits in the sun and dreams of a truck wondering how he can make one. It occurs to him to make one from the construction set, his tongue at work too within his cheek as he fixes on the wheels. Because he no longer has a truck, he thinks of one and is moved to compose one for himself.

But this is only Muskie. As it happens, when a parent brings us a box of trucks to help us along, and jeeps too and airplanes . . . I have no need to hide them. So satiated are the boys with expensive toys they are unmoved. The toys remain in the box. Even war tanks. Can anything interest them at all from the towers of commerce? Where are these boys in the morning, the ones who are missing? Out in the snow, digging, hammering with real hammers and real steel nails, some up the school mixed in with senior science and math, or acting pirates in the library. Captioning their own imagery in action. Where are Zed and Henry and Agar? Living out a bombing raid behind some closed door with no planes, no bombs, no enemy. Yet in mind they do have planes and bombs and human waves of enemies . . . exercising their imagery, interested. Their favorite media are never the paint and even the timber ends but the sand, water and acting. You don't see these boys building but you often see them reading, and although Henry is only five, Agar six, they can read as well as sevens. They just can't write, that's all. In terms of preserving the life of the mind, to be deprived is to be passing rich.

As it happens I am deprived too, in terms of an infant

room. In place of wide high spaciousness where no walls divide children into ivory towers, where our children interflow as family, we make do on board a spaceship segmented into cabins. In place of an accessible piano and erupting exploding dancing, we often go in for squabbling. Not at school but at home, or walking uptown round the picturesque corners, I dream of what I haven't got, of what I wish I had, and wonder how to go about getting it.

In mind only, I see a place on the fringe of the town with trees and a hill nearby, and a building there attuned to the scape, broad with a rearing roof. At one end of the length is a glassed-in wall backing a hooded veranda, from which a ramp slopes down gradually to the place where children play. Out there on the grass is a generous heap of not too heavy timber, close to a shed with a lock on the door housing real tools: real saws, hammers and thousands of nails and spades to dig in the bank.

Why the ramp? Much of the equipment is wheeled outside and back in for the night: water tank on wheels, sand tank on wheels and the mud container. The easel can be wheeled outside too when the day is fine; the paint, water and brushes table and the construction set to build with.

There are steps to the veranda, of course. Across the veranda the glassed-in wall, folded back in summer, closed in winter, yet permitting the light and the needed sight of the wide white outside. Inside is a large and spacious room, tall-ceilinged and abounding in air. Wide windows open up the other walls, low for the use of young children, and the floor is bare so they can hear the sound of their own steps; a living sound like children's voices with meaning and rhythm in it.

From the walls jut several mobile screens forming open alcoves: one for reading, another for writing and two for science and math. One is a place to play house in or assemble a playshop in and another a corner for pets. There's a piano in one, a good guitar and other musical instruments.

Three doors open off the three walls: one for a porch for their clothes and lockers and a toilet compound, a room at the back with a concrete floor for cooking and kiln work, and the third is a room where teachers go to regroup their faculties; to review the last hour, conceive the next and to think in privacy.

Only well-trained teachers work here, both men and women, and in the style of the future. Dead grades give way to interflowing movements from the reception class up. Each teacher knows each technique of each of the four movements, though responsible for his own, so that any child has access to any teacher in family fluidity.

Not only teachers are here but the whole range of life, from a baby to age, maybe a teacher's baby. Maybe an old man snoozing here to be considered and passed his paper and, like the baby, not to be waked. It's a dream just as vivid as Muskie's when he hasn't got a truck.

I'm not the only one writing books for children; they're writing them for themselves. Peter writes over a span of days:

> *"My Daddy."*
> *My Daddy is*
> *in Europe.*
>
> *My Daddy came*
> *back from*
> *San Francisco.*

> *My Daddy went*
> *with us ski*
> *team.*
>
> *My Daddy's*
> *going to*
> *work here.*
>
> *My Daddy went*
> *to Dallas.*
>
> *I love Daddy.*

Odile writes as the snow is falling early in November:

> *"My Cat."*
> *I have a cat*
> *named Demos.*
>
> *This morning*
> *I was sleeping*
> *in a sleeping*
> *Bag and Demos*
> *came up and*
> *scratched*
> *me.*

And another called

> *"My Brother."*
> *When it is my*
> *brother's birthday*
> *I get to sleep*
> *upstairs.*
>
> *My brother has*
> *a new race*
> *track.*

> *My brother letted*
> *me play with*
> *his race track.*
>
> *My brother*
> *is nice.*

Isadore enlarges on what she said before about not wanting to work:

> *I I I I*
> *Don't*
> *Don't*
> *Want Want*
> *to to to*
> *do do do*
> *Work Work*
> *Work Work!*

(in case we didn't hear the first time).

From Grade 2, "Blue Bird."

> *One Small*
> *blue Bird was*
> *Born one day*
> *the mother*
> *died So the*
> *Bird lived*
> *on and*
> *on and*
> *on*
> *and*
> *on   the end*

A story we like comes from Grade 2, called:

> *"the butterfly*
> *without a name"*
>
> *One Day Birth was*
> *made. to a Butterfly.*
> *the Butterfly could*
> *not name her Baby*
>
> *She thought of Willie*
> *Barbra Jane Freda and so on*
> *finly she named her Baby . . .*
> *butty!*
>
> *Butty was a nice*
> *Little Butterfly*
> *She was Sweet*
>
> *One Day Butty*
> *was in her*
> *favrit tulip She*
> *got tird of it*
>
> *to her surprise*
> *she had a baby*
>
> *here we go*
> *agin with*
> *Butterflys!*

One day Zed Zane writes a serious novel, but not at school. Not about gladiators and gunships but about something he loves:

THE ADVENCHERS OF ZEDDY AND FRESHY
by Zed Zane

ZEDDY AND FRESHY
Freshy was Zeddys dog.
When zeddy gets up in the morn.
freshy jumps up on him.
Freshy chews on everything.

Bonny was zeddys little sister.
thay play with freshy a lot.
sometimes zeddys daddy says
he will kick freshys head off.
(sometimes he dos)

freshy yels a lot.
freshy bites a lot too.
Now I have told you
about zeddy and freshy
Now I will tell you about . . .

THE ADVENCHERS OF ZEDDY AND FRESHY.
by Zed Zane.

these are non-fiction stories

It was a long day
and zeddy went to the store
to buy freshy a loleepop

he found 2 loleepop.
he also brot a bruch
and some fome
to clean up his messes.
after that he went home.
and thay played toogether.
the end

WHY FRESHY CHEWS
When Zeddy got freshy
he was sent a blancet
for him to chew on.
like the loleepop
zeddy brot for him to chew on
the end

FRESHY.
As I said
freshy was zeddys dog
freshy chewed and bites
and yells a lot

(last page)
all those pages were good
whert thay.
Your probulee going to say no.

ITS TIME TO SAY GOODBY. GOODBY
What am I saying?

THE GIANT DOGS
One day freshy and zeddy
where wallcing down the road
when two horses came.

Freshy thot thay where giant dogs
so she ran back
to the house
and hid under the car.
THE END.

Rocky is brief, as poets are:

I'm happy.

*Clouds are
happy.*

*The ducks
are coming
to school.*

*A girl is
coming to
school She's
bringing
something
that sings.*

*Racoon by
The acorns.*

One day, writes Candy,
*there was
a person
he was
very poor
because
his wife
was lost.*

Interesting. Why should he be poor because his wife was lost? I can see a wife being poor because her husband was lost. No doubt the husband will go out and get a job. Might even take over his lost wife's job. Still it's sad to think of his wife not round to keep this person. Modern, of course, but . . . and when you come to think of it, why not? Why shouldn't his wife keep a person? This person might have some thinking to do, whereas thinking takes time. And his wife might as well make herself useful.

One day, on the next page of Candy's book, swiftly illustrated,

> *he*
> *went out to*
> *look for his*
> *wife.*

I hadn't thought of that, you know. Which is really a better idea. Go and find this lost wife and haul her back. Send her to work again so he'll no longer be very poor. To be poor is all right but *very* poor is another thing. Very anything is suspect, presupposing variation, whereas nonvariation, leaden monotone, is the passport for the cosmos. Variation uncovers feeling, confesses imagery, which at once classifies Candy. Plainly she's not heading for the super-planet light-miles out in the cosmos but will be left living on the earth amid hair and hearts.

> *One day it*
> *was a rainy*
> *day.*

Rain. What a moving word. Rain. Cloudbursts of love descending in silver sound, so that water and tears drown the eyes. Freshness leaping from the soil with cells dividing greenly. Shade you get from pluming plants, from friendly foliage; shelter and metaphor. Poetry bursts from things that grow, needing the analogy of nature.

"One day," she writes, "it was a rainy day." The day the person set out, presumably, to look for his lost wife. What a rich person, Candy's person, having not only a purpose, somewhere to go, someone to look for, a want, a deprivation, but a rainy day to search in. In the illustration there's a look of yearning in his eyes, anxiety in the line of his lips and the rain drips from his hair and lashes. Where shall he look for his wife; has she wanted her freedom? Doesn't she know that freedom costs responsibility, that love costs sacrifice; does she not have feeling to inform knowledge which is wisdom? Maybe his wife has streaked to Cosmet, the super-planet, and is growing flowers from her brain. No doubt her body is slender-lengthed, her legs superb, and her breasts straight from a brassière ad. Her eyes will be languorously lazy, sapphirine, and her tongue like stretch-pants. A talker in multimonotones. You'll have a long way to go, dear person, looking for your wife. In fact, you do not qualify at all with your feeling and imagery. Better break branches to make a shelter and let your whiskers lengthen.

You should see the size of Candy's raindrops in the illustration: bigger than the man himself, who is on a horse. Each drop alone big enough to encompass man and horse.

> *One day*, on the next page,
> *there*
> *was a*
> *very*
> *lot of*
> *bulls.*

Conceivably. Frightening propositions. Alarming possibilities. Perhaps he doesn't really want her at all. Perhaps he misses her only because the textbook psychology declares that he should be missing her, and if he had not gone through university and passed his crushing exams, had he known nothing of the miles of textbooks on miles of psychology, he would have felt rather than thought that he needed her or didn't. Maybe it's not important about the size of her breasts, the length of her legs or the slope of her luminous eyes. Maybe it is more important that she know how to love so that their sex exchanges took a day rather than a minute. Is it possible that sex is not independent of love, but part of it? Indivisible from it? If so, where was her love? Did she love or, put it this way, *could* she love?

Another of Candy's very lot of terrifying bulls faces him: have I not been urged by commercials and advertisements and endless talk on the campus that legs are the crowning glory of a woman? The bulk of a breast, a tight vagina? What if I have been wrong all this time, he reflects. What if my wife is actually no more than brains on a pair of legs? What if all this time courting, winning and living with my wife I have been missing the elixir of life itself. that which goes between one and another?

There are three lethal bulls in Candy's drawing, blowing fire and smoke from their mouths reaching to the sky, and with horns like carving knives.

This person pauses in the pouring rain as he confronts them. And as he stares them out in his desperation they become nebulous, then shadowy, then mere suggestion, until they no longer exist. He knows that he need not seek her, while Candy writes,

> *One day*
> *there was*

a very
lot of flowers.

The flowers she has drawn all through the writing, weaving through the petals. Gay blooms of expectancy of the kind which could never grow on Cosmet. They are creatures of rain, the flowers, born from the soil and the seasons' rhythms. Their faces are petaled in hope, symmetrical with the pride of fertilization and in-held seeding. Like the face of a girl proudly pregnant to a man she loves. This a page of an earthener.

The rain has stopped and the sun is out as the person looking for his wife because he is very poor sits on a bank to dry himself. What a good thing she has gone, he is thinking. Had she not gone, I'd never have known that there were flowers like this in life. He reaches forward and touches one but does not pluck it, and as his fingers feel the petals raindrops sparkle on them, some to fall on the grass. Finally he stands, shakes the wetness from his hair, brushes it from his beard and returns homeward.

One day
it was
a very
disturbing
day.

Candy is heavy on the "very." A word of the Earth. Here is a drawing of the person sitting in his rocking chair, but he is far from relaxed. He sits upright with his arms outstretched to a smaller someone standing before him. Obviously there is dispute between them. It looks to me like the generation gap. It looks as though the little someone is insist-

ing on showing his (or her) work to the irritated person who
. . . a drawing and some writing . . . who hurls it from
him. Youth trying to interpret itself to its elders, who furi-
ously determine not to understand. But is this generation gap
actually between the youth of the present and the old of the
past, a matter of decades, or between the youth of the present
and the future? Maybe this older person is the future; the
generation gap a matter of hundreds of years. Did I say hundreds? In terms of the stars among which we live, it could be
eons of light-years, the generation gap. In terms of my own
fantasy, put it that way.

The way this youth of the present, because it is present,
is convinced it is the latest and knows the most. As though
reality meant anything in the face of fantasy. What has reality got in common with children? What makes everyone
think, especially teachers, that children live in the world of
the real only? If at all? The irritation of the person in the
rocking chair looks to me to be the irritation and impatience
of the future at the slowness, the dragging steps of youth to
learn the future. This is, as Candy writes, a very disturbing
day.

> *One Day*
> *My Daughter*
> *ran*
> *a*
> *way*
> *From*
> *home.*

So the little someone was his daughter. After freedom like
her mother, I suppose. Thinking that freedom is something
to be snatched. Never knowing, either of them, that freedom

is something to be paid for in the coin of responsibility. Without being paid for, it is no longer freedom but license, selfishness or anarchy. Words of the Earth. Words that cannot occur space-years hence on the new host planet, Cosmet, where feeling is no more than a historic nostalgia. The little someone is migrating to Cosmet too, leaving the person behind on the earth with other like persons, dreaming in multitudes. For no one dreams on Cosmet. No one can dream without imagery, native imagery, and there's no imagery left in the minds of the future Cosmet people.

Dreaming in multitudes. Only eartheners of feeling can dream in multitudes . . . or even conceive the term itself.

One day, Candy writes on her last page, not without relief,
We WenT
To — The
circus.

We might as well. Whether dreaming in multitudes on the Earth or out there among the stars.

A great dark sleep
has fallen on life.

—PAUL VERLAINE

November, with the snow soft and thick, the days short and white.

Where are the instincts? Where are those fear and sex words, the love and hate? I wonder if that "hairy gorilla" of Peter's was a symbol of what frightens him? When was that, now? Back in the second movement. The way his glowing eyes dilated as he spoke it to me, gazing ahead of him at something I could not see. I wonder if many of these Halloween words are in fact symbols of what they fear without knowing what? "Hairy gorilla," "wicked witch," "wild buffalo," "devil" . . . "spook." Could this be why Halloween so carried them away to the point of mob rule—fortunately a pleasant mob rule—when they took over the school that morning for their party . . . fear channeling out? I wonder.

Sitting among the passing legs in the hall, I decide to make yet another qualification of the application of the organic formula to suit these children. Until now I've never had to wait long for the words "love" and "hate," but now I'm sick of waiting. I determine to outright teach them, which elsewhere, in my view, would be sacrilege. Before I start, however, I use an unfailing catalyst, a word which was responsible for opening up to me decades ago the whole astonishing area of the imagery, a word I used accidentally: "kiss." Shivering excitement possessed the children of a race at the tail end of civilization on the appearance of this word in school. Once seen, never forgotten, representing as it did the second most powerful instinct: racial preservation. A word to be returned to, stared at, spelt, turned over in the mind's fingers. "This word is 'kiss,' " I say casually, writing it on my paper.

They look at it curiously, academically, but unmoved. "It's got two esses," Rocky remarks.

And from Odile calmly, "I can make a 'k.' "

Kiss failed! Now Candy drifts by in the white lace dress trailing on the floor about her, saying over her shoulder to me, "Getting married." Later it comes out on paper drawn with crayon, the detail of the "getting married," nothing withheld, at which a few glance as they would at anything else, but there's no giggling or shock. I'm the only one who is shocked. I get the feeling I am ringing up someone all the time but the phone is continually engaged.

"This word is 'hate,' " another day writing it. "I know what I hate," but don't name it.

"I hate Larry," suddenly from Milly, who seldom speaks.

"Who's Larry?"

"He's at home. He's four. He hits me."

These little brothers again. And this the little girl with the tender K.V.: "baby," "doll," "cat," "Milly . . ." one of only two with their own name. Then "my puppies," "my feet," "my dog," "baby guppies . . ." her concern for small beings. Teased by this younger brother. This ever-surfacing accusation, the teasing brother.

Odile says, "I don't hate anyone," and doesn't use the word.

Candy's not here, away getting married.

Rocky explodes terrifically, "No, I don't hate anyone either. I just hate being late."

"And I don't hate anyone either," from Gelo, sincerely surprised. "I just hate it when someone breaks my clay." Legs pass between us.

Peter's intense eyes lift. "I hate my brother."

"Why?"

"Because he hits me."

"Is he younger than you, Peter?" looking round a leg.

"No, he's bigger than me and he hits me." Another of these brothers. At least the instinct to tease remains intact.

The word "hate" isn't used again in subsequent writings. Can you believe it? We could be inbreeding the perfect character.

The third movement had started off at Halloween time with five or six little children, and now I find myself making more little blue books for others floating up my way: Milly's brother Jacky, older than she, who comes to us at

seven, which brings up this pleasant point about children
starting later; in no time they catch up with their peers, finding the preliminary work easy. In no time he's slipped
through the K.V. and second movement, and is smiling away
in the third. And what a boy for smiles. And I make a book
for the vital Durla, with energy enough for four or five and
good will enough for dozens. Sometimes the elusive Isadore
is with us, but more often with Carl or the others. If anywhere at all, she's with Grade 2, which suits her socially
though her tiny hands find writing punitive. Actually, the
way she holds her pencil . . . have you seen it? Who could
write holding a pencil like that? Besides, Grade 2 go in for
exuberant plays, and this is what she just loves. But
wherever she is or isn't she's welcome.

Agar has joined us lately, and Henry, for Zed has
moved up to Grade 3 in the upper school, for how long remains to be seen. And Carter of seven has caught up effort-
lessly, having had no reading or writing before he came. In
some ways it doesn't hurt to start at seven, but not in all
ways. It depends on who it is. "You're the best boy writer in
the world, Carter. When you're the best boy reader in the
world too . . ." and he smiles with pleasure.

There're quite a few of us in the corridor now and the
highway is cluttered somewhat. But no one minds; I like it
myself. What I like most is being so accessible to everybody,
not only to children and staff but parents and visitors. As I
say, I have a natural disposition for international air terminals and interplanetary intersections. It's the life you get
mixed in. People.

Temperatures outside are touching below zero, midway
December, before the fortnight Christmas break, and I'm

having a look at my record folder seeking something happening. I've cleared a table in the math room now, which is my new place to be found, having had enough of the storeroom . . . and a place for teachers to come and rest.

My record folder. Since the flop over the word "kiss" and the blank which the word "hate" drew, I haven't taught the word "love," as I'd meant to. I'm not sure why but it might be because one resists rubbing out . . . erasing, I mean . . . one is reluctant to erase the last hope. As a hope I let it lie.

ODILE'S LITTLE BLUE BOOK READS: *I'm a duck, playing barbies, my own pillow, my Dad's picture, Red Riding Hood, full of candy, my blue book, my snoopy doll, out the window, climb ladder, my brother's big, my Daddy had a birthday, I read my cards, I'm going skating, playing house, you came Janet Waring* (mother), *played.*

Her record feels like firmly woven texture, with no leaks and loopholes, no holes or looseness. Sound. She's able with a pencil or magic marker . . . the speed at which children draw! No second thoughts, you know. Bang, hit, miss, and there you've got it. Astonishing to watch them. I like watching Jonathon draw on his blackboard, the deliberate certain way he goes about it, as though his man were already drawn and he was only tracing it. Starting from one foot first and working up. No erasing or revision. The assurance, the confidence! And little Muskie also. The two of them sitting together on the floor of the meeting room, a blackboard apiece, heads down. Afterward I take these chalkboards and stand them on the chalk ledge on the wall. . . .

CANDY: *I got money, I like clay, our flower pot, I like my sister, Blue Legs, she dropped it, I love you, getting married, meeting time, type three letters, acorns everywhere, I have a lot of money, I didn't, Chaser knocked down a bag of noodles, I know where your house is, I like to play with cards, Odile came over to my place three times, I'm going to have a horse.*

I note the first use of the word "love," surfaced by itself, and all which this tells, but then Candy was a recognizable original from the start and it's from these originals we . . . I, anyway, take my leads. Gelo often gives me a lead: the way he takes off outside to play helicopters on the big rock, dig forts, build bridges. And little Bonnie and Jay, the way they crawl off up-ship to the senior end, playing kittens in and out of the office and under their tables. They show me. You could all but say they do my thinking for me when it comes to directions and interpretations. I get down on my knees too and play kittens under the office table, as I follow on occasion Gelo & Co., Zed Zane and friends; these demonstrate free of charge, teaching me the powers of imagery, how it operates —the direction finders.

Yes, oh, yes. Candy's simple "I love you." Well in advance of everyone else . . . indeed, the whole of the warmth and feeling in her writings: "I like clay," "I like my sister," "I know where your house is." As for the "type three letters," I remarked one morning as she stood beside me with her little blue book, yawning, "I notice you're sleepy."

"A-a. I was late getting to bed."

"Oh?"

"I had work to do. Letters. I had to type three letters."

It gives me faith, if I may use the word. This is how it

could be with them all. Imagination. She's already writing other books under her own power, at home or alone in the clay room. Very seldom works with a group. Her book "One Day" was done at home.

I had said to Rocky the morning after Halloween, "I saw a lot of you children last night. I was at a friend's place. And all you children kept coming in: devils, spooks, witches, clowns, Mexicans . . ."

"I was a Mexican."

"I didn't see you come in, Rocky."

"No," wistfully, "I stayed home."

"I see. The children called at your place, then, and . . ."

"No, no."

"No?"

"Nobody came."

This poem of his, "Nobody came" . . . Only two words, but a masterpiece of pain. "Clouds are happy" is another which would honor the Japanese haiku, a masterpiece of joy. Loaded words which carry so much. "My book talks" . . . the load again, the vision in a boy of five. "Raccoon by the acorns"; this word music in a dim-lit corridor among the passing legs, amid the high sound of small children. But where else would you get it? It's a case of deprivation paying in dream.

ROCKY: *I was a Mexican, Nobody came, Daddy tapes, to New York, Mom is just still asleep, clouds are happy, my three cats, my book talks, my motor cycle, passenger train, I like skiing, my cats jump, raccoon by the acorns,*

> *my cats jumped on my face, I don't like being late, sing freight train, I ate at Carter's place, I'm going skiing tomorrow.*

Now here's Jacky. At seven he would be well past the stage of the home symbols had he been at school. Conceivably he's covered that area at home. His K.V. has been peripheral words. His second movement also:

> *my blocks, two panthers, Panda Bear, pocket knife, King's castle, eat Carl, new house, hay fort, wood house, hitch hike, get out, chalk board, secret fort, ski fast.*

Plunging straight into a boy's interests from the K.V. on, with a steady cohesion of mind like his sister Milly. In their utterances is revealed the integration of their home, the unity. Later he may recall the loves of home, but so far he's been with us only one morning: "Daddy is home."

Gelo is one who gives me leads; he too has written of love, as Candy has; "I love Priscilla." And I recall how adamant he was at the time of "I did not pour the paint in the water." Threatened injustice brought from him the longest sentence he's written in his life, along with the denial about "Jonathon pulled me in the clay room," another time he was on the point of being blamed for something he didn't do. A sense of injustice survives. In his concern at injustice being done to him, Gelo at the interplanetary intersection in our corridor is taking a definite direction . . . and it won't be through space to Cosmet. He does the loveliest, most personal art work whenever he lifts a brush, a crayon or a pound of clay, or when he picks up a spade on the plain.

GELO: *I'm going to be a clown, my guinea pig, playing with sand, Mighty Mouse, my lunch pail, my blue sweater, mine watch, present for Mommy, I love Priscilla, Mr. Punch, Community School, cuckoo bird, Our dog Simon, trolley car, Jonathon pulled me in the clay room, I did not pour the paint in the water, we bought a calendar, We are buying a Christmas tree, a very pretty painting, very nice house.*

I've had a pretty good idea all along who poured the red paint in the water, making it look like blood. Horribly like blood. Candy's "I didn't," was in connection with that blood . . . the red paint in the water tank, I mean. To her the threat of injustice again. You can remember for a whole lifetime anything unjust, whereas you can forget the just. I know who shed the blood and it wasn't Gelo or Candy. But the surfacing of Gelo's "I love Priscilla" and Candy's "I love you" makes me think I might risk teaching this word "love" before any of us is much older, and I may not be disappointed.

And here's another with us from the K.V. and second movement with a little blue book now: Durla, but only just arrived and with nothing written yet in it other than her name on the cover. But you should see this cover, all drawings: a night landscape in silhouette, yet the sun in the sky . . . going down, I suppose, and something else in the sky that may be a kite, and her name, Durla, with a frame round it. She's like a race horse dancing round at the starting line, radiant to get going. Durla has three jobs assigned to her name, a meteor on course. She can't wait and neither can I.

She was one of the few who started off in the K.V. with home words, two: "baby" and "Manly," before losing touch, though there's a fairly cohesive feeling in her two-word captions, as though she were settling after the rickety start. Anyway, here she is with us now in the corridor, book in hand, spark in eye, missing nothing whatever. Still sitting at the table near the window, I look at her second movement.

DURLA: *new blocks, Indian costume, donkey pocket, my blankey, flower pot, Dolores Rick, gun shot, Hamish Rick, Mark Rick, tunnel, garter snake, don't touch, angry, hippopotamus, cookie pot.*

PETER: *Trick or treat, a big boy, I like writing, I like to play water, My Daddy went to Dallas, my brother hits me, the captains, Hatty makes me mad, I'm not frightened, I am last, help me think, barking at people, I'm six in four days, my Daddy has a new baby-sitter Wilma, My Daddy cut one piece of bread, my three books, my snoopy dog, there was a fire next door, I was drawing a picture.*

Daddy comes up three times but only in the third movement. No mention of Daddy earlier, so that this is the first movement back toward home loves, however faint, which reinforces my sense of movement in the feeling of these particular children, in some of them: the ones I have accompanied from the K.V. up. Peter was the one who corrected me when I used the word "love." "Not love," he rebuked; "*like*." "I like writing," "I like to play water"; things, not people. Activities of his own. Yet Daddy comes up three times. How much this record folder tells me , , , not least that Peter has a birth-day on Monday.

I include Isadore, another who gives me a lead in the way she operates the desired family fluidity not yet achieved with the rest of us on account of the carved-up architecture and other circumstances. Isadore chooses just which teacher she'll work with if she chooses to work at all. If Isadore can, why not we others? How I dream of this fluid intermoving I've known in the past in a large be-anywhere room. Isadore reminds me of it, living outside of space and time as though walls and clocks were lost. To live like this is a gift. I read her third movement.

ISADORE: *I like Agar, I like dancing, I went swimming, I threw snowballs, the end, I like yellow, the bus stuck, sparkling deep snow, new pony, bag of noodles, paper clips, no Henry.*

Anyone who knows Isadore is not surprised to see two boys present, Agar and . . . in the second movement Henry, and not surprised to note very little writing in any case, being a girl with a fascinating tongue and tiny hands. "I like" comes up three times. "Agar," "dancing" and "yellow" is a fair outline of Isadore. And here I'd say are sex words, and about time. Again the lead from an original. Her face, legs, body, the lot are too lovely to be true. I'd have called her Aphrodite.

Sometimes Agar is with us and what he does write is hard-hitting and to the point.

AGAR: *I think that the meetings are too long, Jo is a dumb teacher, I wish we had an empty room, I saw a fish today, I feel sick, The cow said I'm a cow I moo Moos but I say moo, The snow was one inch deep the day before yesterday, I'm going skating today, I feel sick.*

Henry is another brain on two legs, but like Agar he loses his book or he's away somewhere educating himself. I suspect that these two boys are bored with the infant-room equipment and are seeking the real things. What we haven't got is real workshops. On the other hand, Gelo is never stuck for the real thing but supplies his own workshop outside.

Milly writes far more than anyone. Then there's Carter. How many now with me in the corridor? Carter, Milly, Henry, Isadore, Peter, Durla, Gelo, Rocky, Jacky, Candy and Odile. Eleven. Not too many for a spearpoint. It's December now. Two months not counting October, which was formation month in the stern. After two months:

MILLY: from her first word, *baby*, to *You made a new book for me last night.*
ODILE: from *Waring* to *My Dad had a birthday.*
CANDY: *Beverly* to *Chaser knocked down a bag of noodles.*
ROCKY: from *Janice* to *I don't like being late.*
JACKY: *puppies* to *Daddy is home.*
GELO: *bike* to *I did not pour the paint in the water.*
DURLA: *Gelo* to *cookie pot.*
PETER: *Jonathon* to *there was a fire next door.*
ISADORE: *walked* to *sparkling deep snow.*
HENRY: *my birthday* to *After Christmas we go to California.*
CARTER: *hot wheels* to *I'd like to go skiing today.*

So . . . if the ship had to return to earth tomorrow and we all got out in time, there would be some children forever liter-

ate. Reading and writing have meaning for them. Some
might go on saying they dowanna; neither do we wanna at
times, but we keep on because we know we need to. But when
work . . . in this case writing . . . has meaning and interest, it cannot but endure whether we wanna or not. When
the imagery is alive and active, it'll deliver itself anyway in
some form.

Am I satisfied? No. But for a few words from Isadore
and the several Halloween words, I see no symbols of the two
main instincts: fear and sex. True, over the last few weeks
we seem to be getting nearer to "love," yet . . . but for Gelo
and Candy . . . the word has not been asked for; but, who
knows? When I come back after Christmas, I might risk this
word. Casually teach it.

I believe we would have done better with the deeper vocabularies, that our children would have achieved easier access to themselves had we had the recurrent dancing, spontaneous as well as formal, to widen the vent. There's nothing
like dancing—creative, expressive, physical movement—to
music to open up all we've got. Dancing picks up the im-
pulses and inspirations from the spirit itself which sweep
through the mind and out through the body, picking up all
we've got, mopping up anything lying about: spare feelings,
desires and desperations. Dancing to music knows how to
identify and release man's capacity for exuberance and exhilaration, even to ecstasy, which purify and unshackle happiness. Body and spirit marry each other, and their offspring is
joy. Dancing is a language, a composite language of spirit,
senses and body. It can be a language of fine joy or fine despair, telling what we cannot otherwise tell. Dancing com-
municates all.

There are times in the morning when I get up from the

floor and dance among the children briefly on about three square feet of carpet while they sing to Carl's guitar, but there's a reluctance in them to join me. Their slender bodies built for dancing are severely conservative. Though the most unself-conscious children I've known, especially in the plays they make in Grade 2, they are strangely reserved, strangely shy. When they sing the rhythmic songs, no bodily movement accompanies them. No fingers move, no feet beat, their bodies remain unreceptive to what the ear hears or the throat sings. There's an uncrossable chasm between the spirit and the body, as there has been a chasm between their feeling and their writing only now becoming warily bridged. It is their history of listening without response. Like constipation.

I lead them in Maori simple rhythms at times, which children adore, but no more than six or seven of the seven-year-olds make an attempt to join me. Perhaps my own joy does not communicate itself; maybe there's not enough joy in myself to be sufficiently contagious. I do take them to the piano in the foyer infrequently when the upper school is out and teach them short formal dances, which they seem to love, but what I mean when I speak of dancing is a long way ahead of us yet.

Spontaneous dancing intermittently through the work of the morning Output period is what is sadly missing; it's something which could counter the querulousness and release the happinesses and, in so doing, widen the channels from the imagery outward and ease the flow of captions. But this part of my work remains in dream. On board this spaceship my work is fated to be an unfinished thing.

"Mrs. H.," from Rocky, "Peter says he hates you."

    "Who, me?"

    "A-a."

    "*Me* did you say; does Peter hate *me?*"

    "A-a."

    "What for?"

    "I dunno."

    "Will you ask Peter to come to me?"

Rocky goes. I'm sitting at the table in the math room. The book I've completed, School 8, especially for Peter is not Xeroxed yet, so it can't be that.

    For some reason Peter comes, stands in the doorway, his dark eyes like thunder.

    "Rocky said you said you hate me."

"I do."

"Why?"

"Because."

"You must know why!"

"I do." A slight small boy just six. Now his voice lifts in rage and his eyes widen. "Because long ago when you first came and there were kids yelling in the art room you put me out and it wasn't me!"

"It wasn't?"

"No!"

"Oh, Peter, but I was very new. I made a mistake. I'm so sorry. Will you forgive me?"

"No. You kicked me!"

"*Me . . . kicked* you! But you know this is not true."

But it is to him. In mind he sees clearly Mrs. H. kicking him. At six there is still little distinction between fantasy and reality. To him it's true. He sees it. "It *is* true. You kicked me and kicked me!"

"No, Peter, no. I don't kick children. Never. All I ever kick is a nut on the ground at home, I kick it down the bank. It hurt my toe that time too. The nuts at my place are very hard, like stones, and the trees are very very tall. If these nuts fall from the top of a tree in a gale, you could be knocked out. When there's a gale in the autumn and the nuts are falling, we keep our children inside. I was having lunch once outside and a nut struck my leg and nearly broke it. Our children pick up these nuts in the autumn and fill up wheelbarrows, and we pay them so much a wheelbarrow."

"How much did you pay them?"

"Oh, it all depended on the size of the wheelbarrow, or if it were full."

"You can't," he says, "get paid for a whole wheelbarrow when it's only half full."

"A year ago when I was home in the autumn, it was the little girl who picked up the lot. Kirstine. So she got all the pay. Dollars and dollars."

"What did she buy with it?"

"What was it again now? Oh, I know. Christmas presents for everyone. I'm going to Arizona for Christmas, to a friend. What shall I bring you?"

"A cactus."

"All right. I'll bring you a cactus."

An everlasting hope
Rises through the dark sap
To maturity.
—PAUL VALÉRY

From 37 below zero to 73 above, and now my walks are no longer white but a desert brown. White or brown, however, my walks bring thoughts of children, in particular those in a physics building set on the top of the mountains: passengers on a spaceship streaking somewhere, their only luggage the frail, unique human marvel of a mind; and I fall to dreaming in my old way of what a school I knew has been in the past, what schools are now in the present and what they could be in the future. I revise in mind the ease and the rhythm in the shape of the day, the way it breathes out and then breathes in; the expulsion and then the intake in accord with the order of nature.

The organic shape of the morning is a vessel in clay . . . symmetrical, good to look at, exciting to feel, and when it is dried and firm you can relax and use it. You can pour into it anything you like, from the hazards of spontaneity, exhilaration of experiment, to freedom itself of the mind. The vessel can accept all sorts of media and ways of teaching, accommodate the most advanced thinking, as long as it is shapely, dried and firm. Without containment, spontaneity, exultation and freedom of the mind could seep away through widening cracks into license and anarchy, whereas the feeling that his day has a shape, a benign routine, helps our child to responsibility and our school to stability.

The material in the organic vessel of the morning is the native imagery. The first part of the morning is the Output period, during which the captions of the imagery are released through any media we can lay our hands to: clay, sand, water, paint and timber ends for building; paper, chalk, crayons, singing, dancing and playing house; talking, plays and writing books; cooking or drama; conversations and the words of the Key Vocabulary. There is snow in season, a place to dig and timber pieces to hammer; the whole informed by and productive of spiraling thought and action. Release the native imagery of our child and use it for working material or, "Touch the true voice of feeling and it will create its own style and vocabulary," and I add, its fuel.

The second half of the morning after interval, from eleven to twelve, is the Intake period, during which the imagery released earlier on the K.V. and organic writing is used for working material in reading, spelling, phonics, cooperation and discussion, reading local readers, audiencing a play and ending up with a story. Output the doing time, Intake the learning time; Output the breathing out, Intake the breathing in. The organic morning is breathing of the mind, freedom of the mind within the shape of order. Nature has order, so why not we? You see it in the seasons, science and biology, in anthropology, in the passions of man.

The whole day is not organic work; only the morning. The afternoon has a different character, for, while in the morning we concern ourselves with material released, with the native imagery from the mind of our child, now we work with material from outside his mind, ideas new to him. And this time it is we who supply them. He encounters thought he hasn't known before, has a choice of skills he has not already found in himself. He learns crafts he would not otherwise have come upon, reads and has read to him books he has not written himself, and is often taken on outings, summer expeditions and, in winter, skating and skiing. I call this "handing down the culture."

This handing down of the culture in the afternoon is largely the concern of the parent-teachers who bring in their varied and fascinating skills; drama, paper work, math, puppetry and all manner of arts. Some take groups out and away and regularly to winter sports. These projects are a matter of choice, and go on and on and on.

If we don't hand down the culture, as has happened to nations in history when stifled by their own affluence, civilization will return to the dust again, to rocks and waterlessness.

Organic work in the morning, cultural skills in the afternoon. Material from the minds of our children in the morning, external material in the afternoon. The whole day can be a large shapely vessel made out of order, into which we pour all we've got. A shape contoured by benign routine which helps to stabilize, which in turn engenders responsibility. For in making a new kind of school, stability and responsibility are major requirements for freedom of the mind.

To what extent can we accommodate such a dream on board our ship far behind me up on the mountains; how achieve the family fluidity in a close clutch of cabins where walls segment like surgical knives fragmenting a family? Where the spontaneous dancing? Yet do not let circumstance defeat us; at least I have a dream that lures exercising a teacher's imagery, a dream which shows direction ahead and supplies a sense of future.

A style of teaching suiting one nation does not necessarily suit another. A look into schools, Asian and Western, is to see the subtle differences in children and the not always subtle differences. What my apprenticeship in our school is reminding me, as I've said before, is that children differ not only from country to country but from state to state; from city to city and from school to school. Nor is that all; from teacher to teacher and from child to child. Only the organic style, the material coming from the mind of our child himself, wherever he is, whatever color he is, can accommodate him. Only his own clothes fit him.

An alien perceives more in a country he visits than the people indigenous to it. Visitors to my own country see more of us than we ourselves know, and they say it, which we don't like because it's the truth, and who likes the truth in the press?

Especially when it's about ourselves. As an alien, I see circumstances in this country which North Americans often do not see, the first being that you as a swiftly evolving society have outstripped your own educational style by three or four decades, and it could be that I'm generous. You've also, educationally, outstripped your own terminology. I'm finding blanks all the time where new words should supply the new conditions. Old words like deadwood continue to block the light from the new leaves of new ideas, so that they cannot unfold. I find a sepulchral vacuum when I look for a word meaning "personality mutation." We know that mutation is a physiological thing working through genes of one person and out to his progeny, but what about the mutation occurring in the mind itself, the genes of the personality working out into the progeny? Do you know, for instance, about the mutating of the personality at the spearpoint of civilization; that the proportions of the ingredients of the mind are changing, have indeed changed; that some organic qualities are missing; that there is a new man evolving, evolved?

Surprising . . . not to be believed? But I see it in the new generation of North Americans whom I work with every day. Blindfolded I'd still see it.

Another thought I've been walking with ever since I came is what you mean by freedom. I can't refer you to the dictionary, because I haven't got one here; you can't cart books around when you're in transit. But if you do look it up you'll find its meaning is different from license and anarchy. I look into the dictionary of my own life, where I find that because I wanted freedom of my own mind I had to discipline myself. I learnt it young. Naturally I tried the wannadowanna, which led me straight to hells; agonizing no-exits, so that there was nothing else for it but self-discipline. The other day when I used this word to a young teacher from another country, she advised, "Don't use that word 'discipline' in this country. They don't like it."

"What shall I use in its place, then?"

" 'Guidance,' " she said.

I laughed. It wasn't Guidance that got me up early in the morning when I was young, when I was teaching and had a young family too, and had no time to study. It wasn't Guidance that got me out of bed rubbing my eyes to creep in the dark to the kitchen, turn on the light, make the tea and get out my books. I wonder what Guidance says in the dictionary. And what Discipline says. The dictionary of my own life shows Discipline as putting the boot in. And Discipline itself in my own life's dictionary means freedom of the mind. You've got to *pay* for life. Take what you want from life but pay for it. And if you take but don't pay, life will put you in prison where there's no freedom of anything at all.

I'm not talking about putting the boot in where children are concerned in school. There are two kinds of discipline, the outer and the inner.

Then you get what I call the consequential discipline, a little less pleasant but no less effective. "Come to me, Rocky, for your writing."

"No. I'm playing in the sand with Monty."

"Oh? All right. When you've finished playing with Monty, you can come then."

But he doesn't come and I don't call again. Nor do any of us reprove him. After interval during Intake, when we come to the reading place of our own writing, Rocky's turn comes. "But I haven't got anything to read," he complains.

"Well, read what you wrote yesterday or the day before."

"No," from Durla. "We've heard what you wrote yesterday."

"But I want my turn. I wanna read."

"You should have written something new," from Gelo.

I leave it.

"It's my turn now," from Peter.

The consequential discipline looks after itself.

I think of those early mornings in my youth when I rose early to study before the day got you by the throat. The pages I'd turn over of knowledge teaching me, undoing the shackles of circumstance, unlocking the ball and chains of custom from my thinking: Freud, Russell, Herbert Read; the Bible once more, and dozens of poets, so that the poor tied mind untrussed itself and dashed all ways of freedom. Ran madly this way and that through gullies and over mountains, breathing in new air, new panoramas and untrodden lands. When the daylight made me put them away, or the first baby waking, the day looked different ahead and there were ideas in it, solutions to problems and answers two steps ahead. And it wasn't the wannadowanna which freed me.

The wannadowanna has nothing whatever to do with freedom of the mind . . . and everything to do with its shackles.

I often recall what Senta told me about the introduction to freedom when I asked her what ailed our school. The structure should have been brought over with the school, she said, then little by little the freedom. Before they came, they were told they could do what they liked and they're not used to it.

Rocky. Would you like to come to me for your writing . . . or would you *not* like to come?

Before he considers his writing at all, he's faced with a decision to make: will I or won't I? Yet it's not the decision at issue but the work. Why put this wall between him and his writing . . . a decision? He doesn't see in mind the writing itself but an alternative: no writing. True, there is an alternative but let him find it himself. Don't present him with it each time you present to him his work. Rocky, come to me for your writing. Clear. He sees the picture of himself standing at my knee talking about himself, the conference, and it's nice to be called; you're wanted. On the other hand, he'd prefer to work in the sand with Monty . . . all right. Let *him* see the alternative and take it, in which case it's his own affair, and the consequences too. To constantly approach our child with double possibilities, with an alternative, whenever his work is concerned, or an obligation, practices in him the mechanism of doubt. It is no longer a question of here is something to do but will I or will I not do this thing? It's decisions that are the labor. We know the story of some captive in a tower who wants to marry the king's daughter. The king comes in and says, "Put all the fruit you see here on the floor in those cases to prove your endurance."

It takes him all night but he does it. The next night the king arranges another endurance test, which by morning is done. But the third night the king says, "Put all the large fruit in these cases and the small fruit in those."

Each fruit he takes in his hand he considers and decides which case. Is it big or small? He has a nighttime of decisions to make and doesn't complete his work. By morning he's raving and the king's daughter's hand goes to someone else. Meet a man with an ulcer and you'll see behind him a history of making decisions.

Rocky, would you like to come and do your writing or would you *not* like to come? Monty, would you like to put the guitar back on the table or would you *not* like to? Children, would you like to come into school now or would you not like to? Milly, would you like to help me put the papers on the easel for painting or would you not. . . . Carter, will you change the water in the tank or won't you. . . . Peter, would you like to get off the keyboard or would you rather stay stamping on the keys? Bonnie, would you like to pack up the blackboards or . . . Mrs. H., would you like to write this book on education for the future or would you not like to: I would *not* like to. I'd rather go to all those marvelous concerts in the music tent across the meadow, and attend the seminars at the Institute of the Humanities and go into the country to stay with Ondine and entertain visitors here when they come to the door and . . .

Sylvia. Write that book on education for the future and get it to us smartly.

Yes.

Complete freedom is a heady drink which intoxicates the nondrinker: a powerful inebriator. A man who can hold his drink is one who has learnt slowly in small doses, and selectively. He knows what to drink, how much and when, so that the morning after a party when he wakes he doesn't at once pull the bedclothes over his face. Our child coming from any formal school generously given a tumbler of absolute freedom becomes as suddenly intoxicated, and intoxication equates with irresponsibility.

The word "Freedom" can never be uttered unless accompanied hand in hand by the word "Responsibility." It's kinder to keep the lid on a school for a start, lifting it little by little, simultaneously teaching responsibility, until the time comes when the lid can be cast entirely aside and only two conditions remain: responsibility and freedom.

Our school at this point has been born less than three months, whereas I'm told it takes two years for a school to graduate from formality to freedom, but I don't accept this till I've found out myself. For one thing, freedom has something to do with equality, which can also be misinterpreted: equality can deteriorate into authority in reverse, allowing mob rule and a school stampede. For another, this two-year conclusion doesn't take into account the factors of love and rapport between teachers and children; love and rapport themselves deliver a measure of responsibility, as you see in many a family. I'd suggest the time it takes for a new school to settle would depend on the school itself, on the understanding of the teachers and parents of what they were doing, of what they were trying to do. My own feeling is that our children, while only just beginning to taste personal responsibility, do not yet qualify for the brimming tumbler.

So we're all equal. Equal in what? What are children, what are adults; for that matter, what are teachers? Are children young people born more recently, less experienced, needful of care and explanation, or are they born mature and know all?

Are our children automatically lords of creation and are teachers servants, audience and baby-sitters? When we see five-year-olds running round a fire in an open hole where the clay is being fired, running round the edge of it waving sticks with burning paper on the ends, do we sit and watch and admire proudly? Yet I've seen it. When I disarm the children and take them from the fire, this is brutal authority denying our equality. When you prepare carefully an afternoon's program but the whole school dashes off regardless to skiing, is this equality, or inverted authority? All slithers down into the wannadowanna, the religion of some habitable planet. More than once the occasion has arisen, "I dowanna learn."

"Then what do you come to school for?"

"I wanna."

"School is a place where we come to learn. If you don't want to learn, stay home."

"No."

I know our younger children are not ready for the brimming tumbler of freedom after trying it out: the open day of the British infant-room style, in which impulse sees itself out to the finish of what our child is doing, where all is choice and which requires much equipment. No one interrupts anyone else and no one is called to read. You wait till he says he wants to read and picks up a book, in which case a teacher may be requested for help. He doesn't write till he has the impulse to write and takes up paper and pencil. Halcyon. Utopian. The children do learn to read and write, and under their own power, and I love the whole patternless pattern.

But there's responsibility bred in such children by the end of two years; moreover there's the difference in children, in cultures. Here we have a difference to be admitted between British and North American children; in our case, between British children and our particular children encapsulated on top of the Rockies. The British style may actually suit some North American schools, but not this one.

We all appreciate the British open day, and when the snow is thickening and deepening we try it. The first day is undiluted paradise, the pulse of the infant room regular and a wonderful tone. To feel each of our children occupied in some craft he likes best, in the art room, clay room or math room, and in the room where the books and timber ends are. Just to cruise up and down the corridor absorbing the calm of it. No quarrelsomeness. No confrontations. No thought of equality and no authority, as well as no conformity.

The second day is nearly as fine, but you notice a few things: the impulse of some children has blown its top and they don't know what to do next, they don't appear to want to do something next; there appear to be no more resources from which to do something else next, and the impulse appears to have burnt itself out. A little guidance, maybe? I dowanna. But the day is still lovely nevertheless. The seven-year-olds go for playing house all day for the second day running, their improvisations and impersonations not less than superb, and they are joined by younger children. People like Peter and Jonathon are the dogs and Isadore is the cat. Family fluidity wherever you look, impromptu. This is it, you observe to yourself.

But the third day begins showing cracks, and clay is being thrown in the clay room. Nothing whatever has been put away and the media are less available. What I call sky-larking rears, rough play and tearing about, which has nothing to do with learning, and less to do with teaching. One or two have tried to write books, but no one finishes anything which requires effort, let alone sacrifice. By this third day, we're back where we were at the first day of school: intoxication and irresponsibility. The pulse is irregular, the temperatures high, and as for cruising down the corridor in bliss . . . you don't cruise anywhere.

What we miss is the shape. The rhythmic breathing of the organic shape, the routine, the stability, the personal obligation; above all, the daily private conference between teacher and child on the substance of his work, during which the sole attention of the teacher is his right; the passing rapport, the regular daily rapport in which teacher and child exchange confidences; when daily, that which passes between one and another . . . the most important interchange in living . . . blooms; from which are released his native utterances. They're temporarily lost, our children, yet it is from this manifest loss that we realize the progress we've all heretofore made.

Not least do I see the distinction between the British open day and the organic shape of a day; I read that our children are to date a long way off from the total freedom and, most of all, I read more of the character of our children, more of the personality mutation.

Disaster. We can't go on. Like the shipwrecked at sea struggling to reach a raft, we struggle back to the organic shape, which takes much time—a week, at least. It's like starting from scratch again at the beginning of school. And there are days in midwinter with the valley snowed under, when teachers and children can't get to school and the bus gets stuck, when we go it alone again, and the same thing happens. Our children are not yet ready for it. Or suitable material for it, if you like. Our children do not happen to be British children but North Americans at the top of the Rockies; and not only at the top of the Rockies either, but at the spearpoint of civilization. More than that: not a section of humanity on a small island casually merging with the continent of Europe, laughing their way into the Common Market, but the sharp, incisive, swiftly changing, post-industrial, mutating knife-point of evolution halfway to some habitable planet. The style of the one doesn't suit the other.

Working with a young American staff of graduates and never having grown up myself, I'm all agog for further experiment, the next a question of world-wide dimension. In the countries I've lived in, both Asian and Western, I've found up to eighty percent of elementary teachers to be women, also an increasing percentage of solo homes, by which I mean homes where for one reason or another there is only one parent, always a woman. In which case we have our child living at home with a woman, even our child in a dual home from which Daddy is at work all day, coming from a woman at home to another woman at school, from all of which surfaces the term "the woman-bred child." Of more concern is the woman-bred boy, the precursor of the woman-bred man. Take a look at the violences in many societies, the important murders, the sensational assassinations, and you'll find behind them the woman-bred man, with the loveliest manners and politeness. From these solo homes we sometimes, not always . . . no, not always . . . just sometimes receive unsettled children whom no amount of care at school can settle, whatever the able teaching.

As it happens, young men come to us from all over the place: graduates in anthropology, science, medicine, engineering and even architecture. Seeing the point, they try themselves out on the floor with our children, so that the next thing you see them wearing scarves round their necks made of children: children sitting between their knees reading to them or being read to, carried on their backs, somersaulting with them, smelling them, feeling them and insulting them, so that our children find at school the man-woman whole, absent at home, and the desired, yearned-for man-presence. With this domestic harmony at school, we can treat not just the symptoms of an unhappy child but the cause itself.

Not to forget the part about men on the staff working with young women . . . I need not enlarge other than to say it's not only the girls who like it.

Then you get to the part about choice of staff: you've got to be able to read people, before which you need to be able to read yourself, and since I remain a child with nothing to read in myself, I leave the reading of people to others. Living in strange countries and living a long time anyway, whatever the country, should give one reading practice, but I still leave this to others.

Not that I don't know what I want. The first quality to seek is self-effacement, whether natural or acquired. One actually can acquire self-effacement when with children or in the classroom of life. If you mean to learn. You do meet a person who's a compulsive talker and yet a stunning teacher. A receptivity of the other person, an ability to listen, for the other person happens to be our child. When one is unable to make the effort to see another's point of view, I risk being short on tolerance. To add that he needs to be an interesting person might limit the field rather, depending on what we mean by interesting. I won't at this point try the water of this pool. . . .

I don't think it's strange that one meets as many potential teachers outside schools as one does inside. Many a photographer is a loss to a school . . . their quiet examination of a subject, their intake capacity. And gardeners draw small children in their care of small plants and in their thoughtfulness, practiced from long hours alone with the rhythms and order of growth. And, except for the voices of birds, the flutter of butterflies and the friction of leaves in the wind, the silence they live in. It gives something to a man. You can trust a gardener. He comes to be something of a natural philosopher, like butchers and bartenders.

On the other hand, many are the teachers already in class, trained and certificated, even dedicated, who could give more of themselves elsewhere and be valued more elsewhere. You run into people sometimes in a school who have never seen a training college, learning the hard way by experience, face to face daily with the reality, yet teaching exuberantly. And it is terribly hard to learn to be a teacher, whether trained or not. I had five years' training, yet when I met my first class I didn't know what to do about it. It took me years to understand. *Years*. Anything I'd learnt in training college seemed to mean nothing. Though it must have. Since then, I've found out for myself that teaching ultimately depends on this something that goes between one and another; this same something which goes between one friend and another, between any one person and another. The greatest events, as well as the smallest, come from this personal interchange, this relationship; rapport, I suppose, though you can get sick

184

of this word. None of which you learn, or know you are learning, or benefit from learning in college. For before you become a worthwhile teacher you need to be a worthwhile person, whereas becoming a worthwhile person takes time. Professional poise is about what it amounts to.

At the risk of being obvious . . . at the obvious risk of being obvious . . . I still suggest that on the choice of staff depends the relaxation of our children; relaxation at least allows happiness if other conditions are present, while happiness itself does help us along in the nursing of responsibility, the coin to be paid for freedom.

All that we're going to do. Dreams flare in the sunrise of hope. Keep the education of the future up with the new people of the future, and to keep up with the future a new vocabulary of the future. Much obsolete terminology to be chain-sawed and strikingly replaced. It has been in most other, many other vocabularies, so why not in education?

This term "Head of Department," for instance, how does it interlink with "All Are Equal?" As things are, you can find yourself appointed director of a program, not necessarily in a school but in business and institutes, yet simultaneously required not to direct, since all are equal regardless of experience, and none likes one to be above the other. Conferences and pooling of ideas democratically can be hours passing pleasantly by, maybe better socially and very very equal, but what about the original vision? The action finally taken can be far from it. Vision does not come segmented in many attractive packages but explodes in one mind alone, and is fragmented and defused when all are equal, which in practice turns out to be "All Are Authorities."

Of "Head of Department" and "All Are Equal," as

terms, one needs to go. The former, I'd say. In mind, I use the word "conductor" in the text of an infant room, as of an orchestra where many playing together interpret one work, led by the vision of the one composer. I do not recall seeing orchestras in rehearsal stopping for pleasant conferences to change a passage in the music since all are equal and have *every right*. Besides, "conductor" concerns itself with something living, with unity, shape and rhythm; with a common intention and, above all, wholeness . . . none of which you are likely to see in "Head of Department."

In the place of "grade" I've settled for "movement" myself, as movements in a symphony or sonata. As I've said, I resist the word "grade" when applied to children. We grade fruit in New Zealand, frozen mutton and wool, but not our children. The word "movement" is more attuned to living creatures who change vibrantly, abundantly. A movement is an organic part of the whole, indispensable. Movements of children from four to seven: first, second, third or fourth, according to how things go. Even fifth, if necessary. The first movement I call the reception, where a senior teacher first welcomes the new ones, a high skill in itself.

In the profusion of growth in education, a term needs to prove itself in keeping up with change; to be as flexible, mobile and as open-minded as the young people it describes. The idea of movements is the source of the word "conductor," for it's the conductor who unites all movements and relates one to another.

And why can't we call a child a child instead of a pupil or student? "Pupil" was used in Dickens' day and what is a student? Has it got arms and legs, tears and smiles and a mind with mystery? "Kids" used to be the aptest word, and still would be had it not gathered irritable overtones. Those damn kids! A pity. "Children" is a word which has stood up to what the years have thrown at it and come out heroically constant. In the probing and spearing of swift evolution, some words can take it and some cannot; it's the way a language evolves.

Other words are up for sale. . . . "Lecture" is one which has had its deadening day. "Teach" has been abused almost beyond its meaning, and so has the word "school." I can't coax my legs to walk out the gate if they think they're going to school. I find myself saying, "Now come on, legs, you're not going to *school;* you're taking me to a place where children are, where we're likely to have a good time," upon which they consent to move. I don't know that "seminar" and "workshop" can hold out much longer, either, while "convention" is morgue material.

"Class" and "group" and "lessons" . . . it's the overtones of the past haunting them. What we want is some Latin or Greek scholar to sit down and compose new words for us before we borrow from other vocabularies. Compose new terminology as they do in medicine, science, astronomy. As the young people do prolifically to accomodate their own style. But since we're concerned with living material, no less than juicy children, they'd need to be living words. No more of "underachievers," "para-professionals," "socioeconomic frustrations." Abstractions! Perishable goods. A little more poetry recalled to the language and picturesque metaphor . . . a mere finger of air writing with silken signature. Divine continuity . . . forgive me.

"Listen, Bill," to a friend from Florida, "we need a new word right here. What shall we have for a person mutated?"

Thinks a few moments.

"Mutation and personality, to be joined together."

Another few thinking moments, then, "Mu-person."

Muperson. Making three to date: Conductor, Wanna-dowanna, Muperson. Oh yes and Movement in place of Grade. After all, *somebody* has to make the language.

Soft-pedal for a while the "isms" and "ologies," the "iates," "ians" and "ists" rampaging through education, we suggest to our word-composer. Our words do not need to be cardiac but at least respiratory. How much longer the words "feeling" and "creative" can take the assault upon them I don't know, but they may turn out to be timeless, on the Earth if not in the cosmos. Maybe they'll last as long as life, for that's what life is: feeling.

These days . . .
Have thirsty roots that penetrate
The desert soil. . . .
They will never cease to try
To uncover the deep wells
For which the heights cry.

——PAUL VALÉRY

Back to 40 below, the receiving snow, the temperatures the lowest yet. The mountains excluding, pocketing, enclosing ensuring privacy as we work.

Back into the swirling vortex of the crowded corridor: to my left the painting, sand and water; ahead the highway room where Carl and the K.V. children are, the timber ends and the books; to my right Grade 2 preparing a play to present late morning; behind left and right the math and the clay room, active with articulate children, and at my feet with me the blue-book children—some of them, anyway. There's much interweaving, inter-roaming and interchange as they compose their own fluidity without dreaming it up first, and much passing by and through of other people's legs and feet which never brush or tread us.

Isadore is with her friends making the play, Candy is composing in clay, Bonnie is off playing kittens with Jay, Gelo is out in the falling snow with one or two associates and Agar and Henry are missing. So is Carter. I know where all of them are.

It's time to print the word "love" on my blackboard. "Anyone know this word?"

"Have," from Rocky.

"No. It starts with 'L.' "

"Last," from Peter.

"No. At the end it's got 'v.' "

"Live!" from Durla.

"Getting warm."

Oh? Gelo back, taking off his parka and boots. "See-see, my hands are cold."

"Like," from Jacky.

"No, but still warm." I'm not giving them any clues; it's their work, not mine.

Milly hasn't spoken but is staring at it, her large eyes enlarging. Candy wrote this word last year, and so did Gelo. Suddenly from Milly, "Love!"

"I was just going to say 'love,' " from Gelo.

We spell it together. "You know how to write 'I,' don't you? Then you put 'love' next to it, like this, and then you put something or someone you love." A departure indeed to *tell* them to, but it's the beginning of the fourth month since we started. I'm sick of waiting for it.

From Milly in time, "I love my dog."

"I love Mommy," Odile.

Oh, here's Candy back looking over my shoulder. "I love Mrs. Henderson," she calls, and looks for her book, which is in the blue box under my chair.

Rocky, "I'm going to play in the sand now."

Jacky, "I love my Mommy."

"How do you spell 'you'?" from Gelo.

Durla has a pencil and paper and takes a long time about it, but she's sure of what she thinks, and knows what it means and keeps going till she's done. "I love my Mommy and Daddy," her longest sentence yet.

"I'm not going to write today," from Peter, but he does. He sits in the arms of one of the teachers, where he writes, "My Daddy is in Europe."

Oh, yes, they use the word "love" today, but will they use it tomorrow? For only one day they used the word "hate."

Tomorrow Milly writes, "My dog shakes hands," and the next morning, "My Mommy drove me to school."

After Odile's "I love Mommy" come "New necklace" and "I've got a new book."

Jacky's "I love my Mommy" is followed by other thoughts: "My Daddy knows" and "I don't walt."

It looks as though "love" is not going to take, either. Gelo first wrote, "I love you," which led to, "I carved wood." Miss again. What about Durla, who wrote so sincerely, "I love my Mommy and Daddy"? "A cayote killed our dog." See? I knew. I shouldn't have tried it. And there I will leave it. And there I do leave it, until Candy comes along with her book, which I haven't seen for several days. After her first, "I love Mrs. Henderson," come "I love Odile," "I love Nell Bell" (mother), "I love Candy," love, love, love.

It is nearly two weeks before the love words come back, as the hate words never did. Milly returns with "I love Henrietta" (baby) almost to the day Odile returns with "I love Mrs. Henderson." Gelo again writes, "I love you" . . . because it is short and easy . . . and another week later others make it under their own power:

JACKY: *I love my dog Bengy, I love my Mommy* and *I love snow.*

DURLA: *I love my guinea pig.*

PETER: *I love Daddy*, but the following week, *I hate Jo.*

As I talk to them one at a time by my side, it is confirmed quite clearly that there is a movement from the outside inward. In their separate ways, in their own time, they're reaching back to their origins. Some of them, at least: Candy, Milly, Gelo, Jacky, Durla and Peter . . . six. People like Rocky remain peripheral where words are concerned; Isadore hasn't been with us over this time but with Carl, Grade 2 or in the upper school exploring upper life. The Three Musketeers, Zed, Agar and Henry, find love the last thing for gladiators and pirates, for pilots and gunship crews, though Agar is not bad at writing short stories which are plainly sex codes, but he writes them elsewhere and not with me, a fact which shames me somewhat. Though he doesn't mind my seeing them, as Candy doesn't mind my seeing her illustration of a man in copulation.

The movement from the outside inward. I'll have to find out what I think about this. Who knows? It might be evidence of some success from our simple treatment of them. I'd very much like to think so.

As the weeks snow by, character and interests become more manifest, so that writings are more worth reading. I notice in Durla's work the recurrence of animals in her busy life: starts in the K.V. with "guinea pig's baby," recurs in the second movement with "garter snake" and "hippopotamus," then runs free in the third, having uttered her love for Mommy and Daddy. "A cayote killed our dog," "My bear is furry and small," "A porcupine scared our dog," "Dinosaurs and dragons lived long ago," "The turtle eats fishes for food," "I'm going to sell my guinea pigs," "I like to ride horses," "My guinea pigs are funny," "I love my guinea pig," "I like goats turkeys and unicorns," "I am going to get some gerbils," "I like bees and bats," "scamper dog," "I like my turtle."

Twenty-four animals at the first count, which is the thing about organic work: the interest in it. Her imagery is alive with creatures, which all but write themselves. She's only five, but look at this.

The movement of Peter arrests me too. None of them doesn't interest me. He wrote before Christmas, "I'm not frightened," but I've heard that before. As he writes on through the weeks, briefly each morning in the highway corridor he writes more and more about Daddy in a way none other does, though coming to it only in his fourth month at school. Daddy is usually first or second to be asked for. "My Daddy went to Dallas," "My Daddy has a new baby-sitter Wilma," "My Daddy cut one piece of bread," "My Daddy is in Europe," "My Daddy came back from San Francisco," "My Daddy has two cars," "My Daddy has a French record," "My Daddy went with us ski team," "My Daddy's going to work here," "I love Daddy."

Peter mentions Daddy ten times, Durla twice. Durla mentions animals twenty-four times, Peter twice, and then not real animals: "hairy gorilla" and "snoopy dog." What he thinks of dogs as a class, real ones, comes up in his "barking at people." He's a boy who uses "I" thirteen times, "my" thirteen times and "me" three times in his writing, with Daddy the great love of his life. Peter refers to himself twenty-nine times and Durla sixteen. Durla is an outward-gazing girl upon the animals which engage her, while Peter is a Daddy-watcher. One cannot miss the character of our child when working organically; it reveals distinctions, the uniqueness of the distinctions and the frailty of the uniqueness. Remember: replacement of the imagery or the murder of it destroys the uniqueness and we've a set of carbon copies.

Odile, as a matter of comparison as well as of interest, refers to herself forty-one times, which is how it is best with a five-year-old, and before I go on I'll have a look at the use of the word "love." It started only late in the third movement, but I'll still have a look at it. Rocky 0, Peter 1, Durla 2, Milly 5, Gelo 7, Odile 13, Candy 35. The variations in our children. Not that these figures prove anything of our child's capacity for loving; some people speak it and others don't. All it shows really is who are likely to speak it and who are not. Which itself is a distinction outlining our child.

Carter, Agar, and Henry have writing, for all their absences, and must have been growing up in their wanderings, educating themselves.

CARTER (seven): *I got a stapler for my birthday, I like Gelo because I like the way he talks.*

HENRY (five): *I am thinking, I feel sick I bumped my head, I am sick today with a cough, How do the people not get killed don't hire them, How do people take pictures of war, We won the war.*

Jonathon has from the start been an interesting boy whose words could never have been anticipated by any teacher or writer: "my bread bird," "my lion," "my Daddy," "my love Jacky," "bike jump," "go crazy," "running jump," "mean Zed," "my Fraser" (senior teacher), "pissy vuna mud," "can't fly," "Hate meeting," "my gun," "my gerbils." He's ready now for a little blue writing book but he stays with Carl. He seldom comes to me for anything, maybe sensing I don't understand him, whereas Carl does. As it happens, I do feel I don't understand him, though he's wholly at home with Carl. So he has his little blue writing book but he works with Carl. He's a boy strongly attached to his home: to his father, mother and baby sister, and he lives out in the country, coming to school on the bus early in the morning, and I can picture how he misses his family for a long day. One day he tells Carl, which gets back to me, that he doesn't want to come to school, which is understandable, though I don't think it is all loneliness for home. He's a boy who goes in for friends, best friends and very best friends, as when he said to Henry, "Will you be my friend? My very best friend?" And Henry, who follows Zed Zane, replied, "No."

But there are others besides Henry, and little Muskie loves Jonathon and I see them sitting side by side with their blackboards, drawing men. I know that Peter loves Jonathon but does nothing about it. I know it from Peter's K.V. But Peter admires him only from afar. I see these heartfelt attachments forming and dissolving among our children, among the girls too, and so do the other teachers, who put much store by them . . . arranging that this one goes with that one because they like each other . . . and I'm touched by it all. No one appreciates the impact of these friendships more than the American teachers, and I learn much from them. In an open school they surface. Not that I am unacquainted with these inter-attachments; it's the intensity of them that surprises me. Sometimes I ascribe them to the strange, hot, dry, loud, contained, overemotional atmosphere in the crowded building, the hum of the furnaces, the dream-like unreality, but other times I allow it is the character of our children themselves, which is new to me—these intense attachments and detachments governing their lives. And it is from these I draw the theme of the series of graded books I'm making: "my friend, my best friend, my very best friend" . . . knowing that our children will identify themselves with the characters, and find reading worthwhile. Noting the quarrels that blow from time to time when an angry boy . . . a hurt boy throws sand, and hearing from one and another on occasion how someone punched him . . . though I've never seen it . . . I use these crises too. What they say is, "He kicked me! He kicked and kicked me!" which I know is not true, for Peter said that about me, that I'd kicked and kicked him. A little girl in tears said, "My mother kicked and kicked me!" Although it is not true, they firmly believe it, seeing it vividly in the imagery. When I have completed School 9 containing these sincere dramas, I think it is mate-rial to be burnt in the marketplace, which has indeed hap-pened to my books before when real drama has surfaced in them, but these may get by here in a school which honors sincerity first and last, in which sincerity is the main status symbol. In any case, I know that Jonathon and Peter appreci-ate these books.

SCHOOL 8.

Page 1: theme words.
   friend

my friend
your friend
my best friend
your best friend
best
your.

Page 2: (picture)
    I like you, Ted,
        Jenny said.
    Ted said A-huh.
    Do you like me?
        Jenny said.
    Ted said A-huh.

Page 3: (picture)
    Jenny said,
    I'll be your best friend, okay?
    But Ted said no.
    Jenny said, Right?
    But Ted said no.
    Why? said Jenny.
    Because I like boys best.

Page 4: (picture)
    So Ted said to Harry,
    Will you be my friend?
    But Harry said no.
    Why?
    Because.

Page 5: (picture)
    Ted went to Bill

and he said,
Bill, will you be
my best friend?
But Bill said no.
Why?
Because.

Page 6: (picture)
Ted was sad.
He played in the sand
by himself.
Until Jonathon came.

Page 7: (picture)
Ted said to Jonathon,
Will you be my friend,
my best friend?
No.
Why?
Because Peter's my friend.

Page 8: (picture)
When Peter stopped by
Ted asked
Peter, will you be
my friend?
No.
Ted said, I'll give you
my orange.

Page 9: (picture)
Peter said,
Will you give me
your orange?

Ted said A huh
Peter said Okay.
I'll be your best friend.

Page 10: (picture)
So Ted gave his orange
to Peter
and Ted and Peter
were friends.

Page 11:
All the new words,
two columns of them.

When I come to revise this book I'm going to use also the term "very best friend." I don't know why I didn't use it this time. Haste.

SCHOOL 9.

Page 1: (nothing on it)

Page 2:
But Jonathon was sad now.
He played by himself
in the sand.
And when he got mad
he threw it.

Page 3: (picture)

Page 4:
But when he saw Peter
eating the orange
he got madder still.

He cried first
    then he punched Peter
and he punched Ted too.

Page 5: (picture)

Page 6:
    Ted began to cry
        and said
    I want to go home.
    But Peter didn't cry.
    He just went on
        eating Ted's orange.

Page 7: (picture)

Page 8:
    Jenny was sad to see
        Ted crying again
    so she gave him a candy.

Page 9: (picture)

Page 10:
    Then she gave Jonathon
        a candy too
    and both the boys
        stopped crying.

Page 11: (picture)

Page 12:
    Jenny said to Jonathon

Why don't I be your friend?
He said
>   *Do you have more candy?*
A-huh.
Okay. You be my friend.

Page 13: (picture)

Page 14:
So Jenny is
>   *Jonathon's friend now*
and Peter is Ted's friend,
>   *his very best friend.*
Now
>   *everyone stopped crying*
and
>   *everyone are friends.*

Page 15: (picture)

Page 16:
Thirty-two new words isolated,
arranged in groups starting with
the same letter.

When it gets back to me that Jonathon has said he doesn't want to come to school, I ask his mother to come in and spend a day with him, and the next thing here is Jonathon reading to her so well and so happily, knowing what he's reading about, especially the emotional involvements of the boy in the School Series tussling with the problems of his friends, his best friends and his very best friends. During the day that Jonathon's mother is here, he doesn't go cruising up-school among the big children, watching them at math, filming, science and the new fish in the aquarium. From all of which I realize again that when our boys wander they learn much under their own power, so that when they do return to the infant room they're not behind in their work at all; indeed, their wits are sharper.

After his mother's day at school, Jonathon settles and stops saying he doesn't want to come to school. I've seen this same solution work before when parents come to school. I know from their writing how much it means to them to find Mommy or Daddy at school. I myself visit the homes of our children a little, so that in the school-home exchange between teacher and parents the chasm between home and school is closed.

As I'm working on School 9 of the series, I consider the children's vocabularies in which I find little evidence of hatred or violence . . . only love. I like to be able to say this about the vocabularies of our children. As it happens, they do their lashing out with their tongues, which, in effect, is much worse, this having more capacity for damage. I've got the word "crying" in this book but I've seen few tears. They are more inclined to lurk and brood with no more than a tear or two. I've heard Odile lift the roof but only when she's physically hurt, colliding with another in the hall, and I've seen Angela weeping passionately over a personal hurt from another's tongue, but she is Angela, the like of whom you'll never find on Cosmet.

Well, it's rather a sweet complaint to make: no hating, no violence but at the expense of feeling. Among many of them there is a surface peripheral life expressed by tongue alone, which I've read from the start in their organic work.

Yes, they've thrown sand at each other, but this doesn't require physical contact. Never mind, they're all very sweet in
my eyes and like my arms around them. Sometimes a girl
will jump up and down in front of me, hands clasped, ex-
cited, and some of them embrace me, all of which well suits
me who has always had a use for arms.

This School 9 is the last I'll make of this series, and
before I return over the nine for revision I enumerate the
favorite nouns they use in their writing and the verbs to hold
in mind as I revise. Not a frantically accurate summary, but a
survey of the writing of fifteen of the children—mostly five, a
few six and two of them seven—over five months. The number of times the words occur:

Own name	6
money	7
house	14
Mommy	26
Daddy	31
animals	90
my	96
I	199

Reference to himself in own name, I and my: 301.

VERBS:	
don't like	2
hate	3
like	32
love	67

Being an alien, I don't read these numbers well. To me, the
"hate" at 3 and the "love" 67 is very good news. Then I no-

tice that animals at 90 is three times as many as either
Mommy or Daddy. One day I tell this to two of the parents
with whom I am dining. "There was 'hate' at 3," I boast
"and 'love' at 67."

But they don't rejoice.

"I like the 'love' at 67," I say.

"No," one replies. "The 67 means a great yearning for
love, which many don't have. The animals at 90 shows where
they turn for love. You see, Mrs. H., many of our children do
not have the tangible love, the cuddles and the kisses, the
presence of their parents. Dogs they can touch and cuddle.
Dogs are warm and receptive. Dogs are very affectionate;
they're always there when the children go home. It's the dogs
they turn to for their love."

Dogs. When I get home, I reach for my summary. Dogs
14, cats 10, puppies 7, guppies 1, other animals 58. But I'm
not impressed. You can't read children by statistics. All I
wanted to know was the word recurrence to use when revis-
ing the books. No, put it away. You don't read children by
numbers.

I think I'll put this School 9 into the hands of Peter first, for
he did love School 8. I think I know at last what attracts me
about Peter . . . mystery. A commodity in short supply in a
people whose main encounter is per tongue. With a minimum of passion the tongue works overtime. At some dis-
agreement with people, you hear, "Shall we talk?" No, it
goes like this: "Shall we talk!" A command. And away she
goes. And so willing are the tongues, so articulate, that the
exercise of reading another's actions, facial expressions, tones
of voice, reactions, drop of an eyelid or lift of a hand, even the

secret twitch of a finger . . . this exercise is out of date
. . . in spite of it being wonderfully understood on the TV
screen. To read another's feelings and motives without being
told what they are, without confession or admission from the
other, does not coincide with overtalk. Reading people's
minds without the talk is halfway to understanding. You can
work this out on the TV screen by turning off the sound
and watching the gestures. Talk, intertalk can be profit-
able, desirable, not to mention enjoyable, but you pay for too
much of it in understanding itself, because so much wording
becomes cheap in no time as quantity devalues quality. Too
much is said which does not need to be said to one practiced
in perception, to one practiced in receiving contagiously the
feeling of another, which brings us back to feeling. Feeling is
almost a separate person functioning of itself, and can travel
from one to another without the support of words. The only
things which need to be said are those which must be said
from an inner compulsion. Too many, far too many questions
are asked which deteriorate into probing, which hurts. It's
best not to probe but to read in gesture, tone and overall response what you want to know from the other, and if you
can't, then at least wait till you're told, in which case you get
told only that which the other wishes to tell, must tell. And
this which one *must* tell cannot be other than interesting and
valuable to hear. The thing is that when the imagery is
alive and active, an idea can grow and elaborate under its
own power from tongue to tongue, can seek and find its own
conclusion, which is the meaning of conversation. Too much
talking, too many questions both defuse the power of the idea
or overexpose it and it's this exposure which is one of my few
enemies in this generous country. The four X's I call them:

exposure, expedience, explanation, exploitation. Along of course with altitude, urgency and wannadowanna; and not just my enemies either but of any nation's. Too much inter-talk—the Meeting, the arena, the inquisition—adds up to this lethal exposure, which annihilates the lure of mystery.

Mystery is a battery which generates interest. Mystery makes you wonder. Mystery calls on your resources of pri-vate divination, inner reading, unspoken assessment; in fact . . . here I am again at the central point of departure to which all roads lead: overtalk atrophies the imagery; mys-tery exercises it.

And this is Peter. Ever a source of interest to us. In place of words, you'll get a look from his dark roving eyes; a lift of one shoulder, a squirm, a smile, an act or a nonact; gestures of stored passion. Or the most powerful gesture of all: silence.

He's never once told me he likes School 8, but it is easy to know it. I've seen these slender fingers of his, the way they hold it. You can tell a man by the way he holds a book as well as the book itself. I've seen him sitting on the edge of a low table, his small knees together, a smile of indulgence and amusement on his face as he reads of the problems of others; of someone else's friend, someone's best friend, his very best friend. It's Peter I'll give this book to first.

After morning interval, the Intake period, and I do put the book in his hands as he is walking into the meeting room, and he takes it with a little snatch and a smile and says nothing. Which is sufficient for me. . . .

It is toward twelve as I sit at my table . . . no, not *my* table but *the* table; *my* table suggests dominance and authority, things or put their own upon them: books, papers, coats, parkas, and the children's things; drawings, math books, puppets, lunches and pop containers, not to mention a teacher's feet. *The* table is far more equal. No doubt I could have my table if everyone on board including every child had a table too, but since they have not, neither have I. Where was I . . . toward noon as I sit at the table in my room . . . sorry, the math room . . . the place where I hang my coat, put down my mittens and keep my snow boots, having had enough of the storeroom, but only because there's no table and chair there; toward noon as I sit at the table in the math room entering notes of the morning's work of one of our teachers who gives us voluntary time, asking him how he got on and how the children were, I become aware of two starry brown eyes on the level of my . . . of the table. "Oh, that's Peter," I say.

Smile; the eyes steady. He fingers the glass bowl of four cactus plants I brought him from Arizona, which he leaves here at school in order to water them once a month. "I'm building a house," he tells me.

"Oh?"

"In the meeting room."

"Oh."

"I'm going to live in it."

"Yes?"

"It's very small."

"By yourself."

"Yes."

"Why, can you cook?"

"Yes."

"And what'll you cook; can you make toast?"

"Yes."

"Cereal?"

"Yes."

"Eggs and bacon?"

"Yes."

"Greens?"

"Yes."

"Can you make your own bed?"

"Yes." Thought . . . then, "The house cleaner will make the bed."

"I see. The house cleaner will make your bed."

"No," thought, "my wife."

"And who will be your wife?"

Looks up and around vaguely, wistfully. "I don't know yet."

It's not till our teacher has completed his report that I see Peter has brought his house and blocks near the table. I hadn't noticed. He must have liked School 9.

Another heavy snowstorm during the night. When I wake in the morning, it is still snowing. I leave home before the light to be at school not later than seven-thirty. The snow is deep, I'm before the plow and there's a slight wind blowing. Walking to school, I know all about temperatures below zero, and I have everything on: warm underwear, thermal socks, fur boots and leather mittens; a woolen scarf tied round my head and a heavy squirrel coat, yet I'm still strangely cold. Soon I stop. Put down my bag and ski pole and add the plastic hood. My nose is so cold I might have to ask a ride tomorrow or do something about covering my face. Yet I'm happy enough as I proceed, and the form of a dog nears me: the snow is no horror to halt my heart; it always warms and cheers me.

The divine continuity
Which does not mark passing time
But rather hides it.

—PAUL VALÉRY

One day the Feds come down from Washington and promise
us a grant. We believe we'll continue next year as a school, as
a center for teacher-trainers. One day there is a very very lot
of flowers.

Our ship is finding direction and pace. We seem to have
come in on some radio beam, directed by some power unseen.
Some claim that the great star increasing in size ahead is a
habitable planet magnetically drawing us in, commander or
no. We start washing ourselves and sprucing up, and where
are our visas and passports? We begin collecting all the
work of our children for evaluation. April it is. Seven months
since we opened, though I never count that first month of
turbulent formation, shaping and stabilizing, which makes it

six. A survey of my records folder not only of all our children in the infant room but in particular what I call the spearpoint children, these which have come up from the K.V. with me through the second to the third movement: Milly, Odile, Candy, Rocky, Jacky, Gelo, Durla and Peter. Eight. And I think on their organic progress.

MILLY: from her first word *baby* to . . . *They want it to be a surprise for Jacky and me.*

ODILE: from *Waring* (surname) to . . . *My Dad is coming back from Chicago.*

CANDY: from *Beverly* to . . . *I love I love I love I love I love I love.*

ROCKY: from *Janice* (mother) to . . . *The ducks are coming to school.*

JACKY: from *puppies* to . . . *I went up the lift with my Daddy.*

GELO: from *bike* to . . . *I love you and I like you and I love Daddy and I love Mummy and.*

DURLA: from *Gelo* to . . . *I like goats turkeys and unicorns.*

PETER: from *Jonathon* to . . . *My Daddy's going to work here.*

Excepting Rocky and his ducks, they have traveled strongly back to the home and most of them stay there. The imagery of home and its loves has awaked. Instead of the flowing from the inside outward, it has been a reaching from the outside inward. To date, as people with minds of three dimensions, as rounded full people, they're safe. But only to date. Yet this is how they would grow if we had them for one more year. And we are going to have them for one more year. It is written. Our ship nears land.

. . .

Most unexpectedly we lose our grant. Our oxygen tank explodes, hurling from the ship pieces of dream which float in space beside us. Look, there's Senta's in fragments. That's mine there about the dancing and spaciousness, the family fluidity. There's yours . . . there's his . . . jagged junk around us, floating flotsam. We must have been too overloaded with dream. All I hear in the white-shocked silence is one parent's whisper: "What will happen to our children?"

Vision answers vividly. Flashing snakes of lightning whistle through the air, thunder tears the human veil and the future takes body. Apocalyptically I see a mutated people, hear the voicemanship of a final race.

On some habitable planet with bleak shadows of rock on sand, dry with nothing growing; abodes bulging tall from the scape itself. Top-heavy shapes, slender and blurred. In the women an inbreeding of lovely legs: long, luscious, languorous. Every limb as far as the eye can see is lineally straight and seductive, all torsos slender-lengthed, drawn by master advertisers. Breasts come straight from the fashion papers selling the latest in bras, sketched and resketched in pencil till they're good enough for ink.

An inbreeding of beautiful faces echoes a precosmic age

on the Earth, beautiful beyond beauty. All eyes lure in sapphirine blues, in amaranthine hues, the eyelids hanging de-
sirously. Not a nose that deviates from an artist's dream, each
mouth as expensively tasty as cool-cotton-candy. Teeth
sculptured in ice, ears pearl crescents, while to look at the
skin is to drink fresh milk sunseted in pink.

Yet are there deviations from the ads. The domes of
their heads are thrice the size of what they were on Earth and
on them, withered by nonstop perming, bleaching, dyeing,
driers and weary wig-wearing a planet ago, not a wisp of hair
survives. Instead, from the big bare scalps, brains protrude
in fetching flowerets which look like high-priced hats—and
prettier than hair, as it happens.

What's wrong with their hands? Only gestures of
hands the size of a baby's, helpless like fins. Nor are these
claws but human fingers with the nails elongated, highly
colored and iridescent; while their feet are so delicately small
you wonder how they function. Cosmic variations from head
to foot, yet recognizably human but for a non-earthly phos-
phorescent radiance. Star material, really.

They talk persistently and simultaneously, meaning
none of what they say, but talk for the sake of talking.
There's an air about it as though each were playing some
well-learnt TV role. They gesture a lot and throw their arms
and stride in pseudo passion. Argument reveals piercing
brain power, crushingly clever but with not one flick of wisdom, for wisdom is inspired by feeling, which vanished a
planet ago; overstimulated into nothing to stimulate. A vocabulary of leaden multisyllabled abstractions holds no
quarter for cadences, while Earth-forgotten relics, memories
of mercy, have dated themselves out. No words for compas-

sion and trust and pity and no syllables for sympathy. The age of feeling is referred to historically only. The Earth Age has swept by as irrevocably as the Paleolithic or Ice Age eras.

In space it's the women who scintillate, for the men seem to be at work all day, making big things with big hands: big abodes bulging from the billows of boulders for their current families. Though the women are tall, the men are small and their hands hang heavily; and though their voices are throaty with ferocious fertility, they rarely speak at all. But by the color of their skin and their physical vigor there appears to be real red human blood in their veins, and it's the men who carry the corpuscles from one planet to another, the haulers of history; for all that the women are good for is to rule and to reign over Cosmet.

Since the women come home only to sleep or eat and the men are away at work, our children have dog baby-sitters; large, soft, loving creatures with hearts of canine compassion who don't require pay. Many are our children who sleep against them, tucked within their forelegs, licked to sleep, licked awake and nuzzled when they cry. Dogs accompany the little ones everywhere, guarding them, mothering and fathering them, for the dogs are the loveliest people to meet, having salvaged human qualities; as animals scavenge for scraps of food, these have picked up loves, loyalties, trust and the capacity for sacrifice, the coin which purchases joy. As the dogs rear our children, they are radiant with joy, rich from the children's affection for them and need of them and from being busy all day with much to do as though the days were worth it. Dogs are the only happy people. While the women are engaged in their latest witch hunt, their newest inquisition or talking on the phone . . . "Now, this is be-

tween you and me only but . . ." our children are lolling at
home with the dogs.

Surpassingly beautiful children to look at, yet these also
have such small hands and feet they can't walk till five or six
let alone do anything or make anything, while their head-
domes also are overlarge and hairless, with brains budding
from the scalps in the prettiest way. And although their feet
have atrophied, their legs still have this exquisite length en-
gendered an eon ago on the Earth, and although their hands
are practically useless their tongues make up for it, so that
they begin speaking at a few months old, eloquently too, and
at length in lucid argument. From birth they learn the Wannadowanna, the religion of Cosmet, from large staffs of serv-
ant dogs, not learning to dress themselves at all or even feed
themselves or to do anything they dowanna; paced by their
brain power, it's their tongues that develop to communicate,
operating independently.

Much of what they do learn, and regularly, is from the
many accessible screens before which they loll from the moment they wake. They talk in high piercing voices to compete with the TV volume, simultaneously, and with an air
of playing a TV role, so that you can't distinguish a TV
role from the living performance. Children engaged in watching the screen are as good as the characters portrayed on it,
so that they often find themselves answering a person on-
screen instead of the one off-screen. The word "love" has
been a dropout from the language light-years ago, as old
hat as military hardware. Sex can no longer be the physical fulfillment of love-that-is-not but perpetuates in the style
of seasonal copulation in a precosmic fowlyard on Earth.
As two smile lustfully one to the other, words twist like in-

valids on their beds, eyes dilating, temples beating, supplication choking in burning throats. Lips mad with thirst come down on lips even madder with thirst, more pruriently dry. Is there no cool dew . . . where is the cloudburst of love descending in silvery sound so that water and tears drown the eyes? The act is executed peremptorily while feeding, talking or walking. A flutter. In, out, and it's over.

In the mythical past on the patriarchal Earth, truth used to be a direction finder, a valid value, a virtue shot with light, but here on this star in the universal order it is utilized as an injection to sedate another to render him vulnerable. Friendships common an eon ago have graduated to sterile alliances based on common blood taste, for the purpose of hunting some doomed other. Blood partners change overnight, overminute when strategy is served. Nor do all actually wish to hunt for blood, but the script calls for it.

Sport on Cosmet is blood, of course, except that it is not the blood of the body they tear from each other but the blood of the spirit, which is in short supply. It is strange that there should be any spirit left, but if there's one thing in man, whether on Earth or on Cosmet, which is indestructible, it is Spirit. Mupersons analyze each other with tongues like pocketknives until they expose the organs, wanting to see inside, what's inside, how it works, to rip it out dripping and display it. "Look what I've got!" they shrill. "Come and see what I've found inside!" Glorying in the flow of blood pain, licking their finger claws and smacking sunset lips. Exposure is the most honored technique. More than words, nothing can kill like eyes.

As it happens, the blood of the women is not really blood but an exclusive iridescent poison, though they like to call it blood. Lust for blood is a marvelous pastime of the man-mechanism persisting over light-years, space-miles, eons and planet-spans from eternity through life to eternity. For, like exquisite legs and glorious faces, the blood lust in-breeds too, as inquisitions, stakes, arenas and homocide repeat themselves like meteors. The blood of each other is the only thing which really interests space-women, who crave the elixir of another's agony as an earthener craved water. It's power they seek over one another, each jockeying for the position from which she can order the lives of others, and power spells out and spills out blood in any culture, even in space.

For there's religion on Cosmet, and religion spells both power and blood. There are three. One endured from the birth of man when he first stood erect on his feet: lying. A second, rather more recent one in terms of space time: the enchanting Wannadowanna . . . I wanna, I dowanna . . . the moral law for all good immigrant mupersons. Entrancing! At last children have the benefit of religion, because they understand it. From birth they're assured that the life to be lived is to be built entirely round what they want or don't want, and to hell with the consequences. Celestial circumstance! They serve the god "I" devotedly. At last they have a credo to live by which is real and which makes radiant sense to them. True it's not an ethic which fruits in joy, but what religion ever did fruit in joy?

The third religion is one which calls you to worship triple gods sitting side by side in a dome: the dollar sign; the

Adman, forcefully visible; and another, invisible—a legendary spirit called Feeling. Having made one's obeisances and salaams and requests to the first two, you kneel fearfully and reminiscently before the empty throne and pray for feeling. Not that you know what feeling is . . . all you know is that something is missing. Something that nothing can buy; that no skill in tongue warfare can win . . . that no face in space can replace.

School is closing. Our ship gyrates. Vision of a habitable
planet of the future, voices and shapes of a cosmic race . . .
the screen rolls down and here is the uproar, the outrage
and uprage of the present. Where are the children? Rocky
and them. Milly, Gelo, Candy and them. Durla and the
gentle Peter? And all of our other children: Mitchell, Henry,
Agar and Zed; Bonnie, Jacky, Jay and Muskie, and where is
Jonathon? Angela, Gemmy, Gerald and Jennifer; Annabelle,
Odile, Monty and Carter, and where is Isadore? Parents,
teachers and dogs?

But all I see are pieces of dreams; severed, segmented
and fragmented. Yet I still hear their voices: Freshy chews
on everything,

Puff the
Magic-Dragon
lived by the
sea

Mrs. Henderson
is in
school

I love my
Mommy love
love love

I love Milly
I love Odile
I love
Su I love I
am Candy

I don't
have a
little book
any more

I went skating
with my
Dad

I like
playing
with clay

I made
caves out
of sand

My guinea pigs
are funny

Monty-my-love

My Daddy came
back from
San Francisco

I saw the
movie of
Lindberg's
plane

Clouds are happy

My   book   talks. . . .

VINTAGE BIOGRAPHY AND AUTOBIOGRAPHY

VINTAGE BELLES—LETTRES

VINTAGE FICTION, POETRY, AND PLAYS

VINTAGE CRITICISM,
LITERATURE, MUSIC, AND ART

VINTAGE WORKS OF SCIENCE
AND PSYCHOLOGY

teaches reading
  by Key - vocabulary
names
    the Daddy, Mommy
  then things

Release the nature imaging of
our child & use it for
working materials